ILLUSTRATED TALES OF
NORFOLK

JOHN LING

AMBERLEY

First published 2019

Amberley Publishing
The Hill, Stroud
Gloucestershire, GL5 4EP

www.amberley-books.com

British Library Cataloguing in Publication Data.
A catalogue record for this book is available from the British Library.

ISBN 978 1 4456 8792 6 (paperback)
ISBN 978 1 4456 8793 3 (ebook)

Typesetting by Aura Technology and Software Services, India.
Printed in Great Britain.

Contents

Introduction

The historic county of Norfolk has more than its fair share of strange tales. From ancient legends, through stories of the supernatural to more modern documented cases, there is much to tell. *Illustrated Tales of Norfolk* brings together all kinds of stories from around the county, including folklore, witchcraft, murder, smuggling, shipwrecks and much besides.

It is virtually impossible to fill a book with tales that nobody has read before – particularly when so much information is now available online. Inevitably, a number of the stories have appeared in print previously but those that are familiar to one reader may be completely unknown to another. Alongside fresh takes on some of the timeless classics are more obscure tales of unusual and unexplained happenings such as the old yarn of the oak tree in the middle of a ruined church that grew from a witch's wooden leg!

The legend of Black Shuck, the giant supernatural dog believed to have inspired Sir Arthur Conan Doyle's *The Hound of the Baskervilles*, probably goes back at least a thousand years and several other Norfolk tales may be as old. Some stories are based on factual accounts, such as Kett's Rebellion of 1549 and the persecution of alleged witches, but inevitably there are different versions of such events and fact and fiction often become intertwined. Some of the real-life stories have acquired a subplot of intrigue or conspiracy and others have strange or paranormal elements attached to them.

Several of Norfolk's historical characters have fascinating stories to tell, among them Robert Hales – better known as the Norfolk Giant – and a Victorian circus owner called Pablo Fanque, who was immortalised in a song by the Beatles. A defrocked Norfolk vicar known as the 'Prostitute's Padre' was mauled to death by a lion. An ancient legend claims that following her beheading, Queen Anne Boleyn's body was secretly buried in a Norfolk church. The county also has unlikely links with ancient Egypt's King Tutankhamun and Native American princess Pocahontas.

Some of the following tales are quite bizarre, but Norfolk can be a mysterious place – particularly after the sun has gone down – and the truth may sometimes be stranger than fiction.

Strange and Spooky Tales

THE LEGEND OF BLACK SHUCK

This is one of Norfolk's oldest legends and certainly one of its strangest. Black Shuck or Old Shuck is usually described as an enormous black demon dog with glowing red eyes and a blood-curdling howl. According to some accounts he has a single huge eye in the centre of his head, while in others he has no head at all! Black Shuck is mainly associated with the Norfolk coast, covering a large area roughly between Hunstanton and Great Yarmouth. He has also been reported as far inland as Coltishall Bridge, just a few miles north of Norwich.

Black Shuck has been seen many times over the centuries, both at night and in daylight, and various versions of the legend give different dire consequences of witnessing the mythical beast. Some state that you will die before a year has elapsed. Alternatively, if you escape this fate then you will have descended into madness before the first anniversary of your meeting has passed. Even if you survive with your sanity relatively intact, you can expect the rest of your life to be dogged (pun intended) by misfortune and bad luck. Some, however, believe that Shuck is a benign and misunderstood entity who materialises to warn of severe storms or perilous seas.

One possible origin of the legend relates to a shipwreck at Salthouse on the North Norfolk coast in January 1709, resulting in the deaths of all crew members of the brig *Ever Hopeful*. It was returning to Whitby in Yorkshire from London when it got into difficulties in a great storm and was beached on a sandbank. The bodies of the captain and his pet wolfhound were found together amidst the wreckage, his hand still clutching the animal's collar and its jaws still attached to the man's jacket. The dog was quickly buried on the beach while the captain was interred in an unmarked grave in Salthouse churchyard. Local people soon started reporting sightings of an enormous spectral dog and hearing its unearthly howls. It was widely believed that the ghostly hound was stalking the area searching for its owner.

The tragedy at Salthouse almost certainly accounts for a large rise in the number of reported sightings in the general area during the years and decades that followed. Some claim the legend has its roots in Norse mythology and may be linked to the Hound of Odin. The name 'Shuck' is derived from 'Scucca', an Anglo-Saxon word for devil or demon. Sceptics dismiss these ancient tales as pure fiction, reworked and embellished over the centuries. In her *Haunted East Anglia*, author Joan Forman suggests that such sightings may somehow be

The legendary Black Shuck is often said to have glowing red eyes. (Illustration by Imogen Smid – www.imogensmid.com)

triggered by 'a racial or archetypal memory, perhaps of a one-time religious fetish or object of reverence in pagan days'. Maybe the 'memory' has faded down the centuries or perhaps those who have witnessed such phenomena now choose to keep it to themselves for fear of ridicule. Nevertheless, quite a few sightings were recorded during the twentieth century and continue to the present day. In her *Norfolk Stories of the Supernatural*, Betty Puttick describes a strange incident when a Gorleston coastguard claimed that 'a large hound-type black dog' he was watching running on the beach 'vanished before his eyes'. The sighting took place early one morning in 1972.

Although Black Shuck is synonymous with Norfolk, similar legends of giant supernatural dogs can be found throughout Britain. Just over the Norfolk/Suffolk border he – or one of his dreadful relatives – is known as the infamous Black Dog of Bungay. It is alleged that the hellhound invaded the sanctity of St Mary's Church during a storm on Sunday 4 August 1557 and killed two

Coltishall Bridge, traditionally one of Black Shuck's favourite haunts.

worshippers. It then went on to kill again at Blythburgh Church that same day. Black Shuck was almost certainly an inspiration for Sir Arthur Conan Doyle's classic Sherlock Holmes story *The Hound of the Baskervilles*. The famous author is known to have stayed at the Royal Links Hotel in Cromer and to have visited Cromer Hall. There he learned of the local legend but was also familiar with tales of similar demon dogs in the vicinity of Dartmoor where the story was set. The Baskerville Hound was therefore probably an amalgam of several shaggy dog stories.

THE HANGING MONK OF ST BENET'S ABBEY

Many places on the Norfolk Broads are rumoured to be haunted and St Benet's Abbey on the River Bure near Ludham is said to harbour a particularly grisly manifestation. The haunting relates to a local legend of betrayal and brutality dating back nearly a thousand years.

Almost immediately after the Norman Conquest, St Benet's Abbey found itself under siege but the massive stone walls were keeping the troops at bay. The monks had a large store of provisions and could have held out indefinitely but a junior lay-brother, who was acting as caretaker, secretly made a deal with the attackers. In return for opening the abbey gate and allowing them in, he would be ordained as Abbot of St Benet's and hold that position for the remainder of

The ruined gatehouse of St Benet's Abbey and mill tower.

his days. The Normans kept their promise and the following day the traitor was dressed in fine robes and duly ordained – before being tied up and promptly hanged. The previous abbot was then reinstated.

The execution is reportedly replayed in full sound and vision on the night of 25 May each year, with the young monk's writhing body dangling above what is left of the gatehouse and his unearthly screams filling the air. The abbey itself is sometimes said to miraculously rise from its ruins before disappearing with the spectral monk. A number of people have claimed to have witnessed this frightening spectacle over the centuries including Charles Sampson, author of *Ghosts of the Broads* (1931). As with any ancient tale there is more than one version and an alternative account states that the monk was 'nailed to the abbey doors and skinned alive'. If you avoid the date mentioned above you may still experience his presence, for he is also seen and heard during dull or foggy days in late autumn or winter. A wherryman is said to have drowned in the river on All Hallows' Eve long ago after seeing the apparition. In his haste to escape he lost his footing in the dark just before reaching the relative security of his vessel.

Another local ghost – that of a man in monk's dress and accompanied by a small dog – has been seen rowing a boat on Ranworth Broad. He is thought to be Brother Pacificus on his way back to St Benet's Abbey. A windmill was built inside the old gatehouse in the early eighteenth century and the ruins are open to the public.

AN ODD CHURCH TOWER AND A SKELETAL VISITOR

St Mary's Church at Burgh St Peter in South Norfolk has perhaps the most unusual tower of any church in Britain. Built around 1793, the tower appears to be constructed from giant cubes of diminishing size piled one on top of the other. It is thought to have been inspired by ancient Mesopotamia's ziggurat temples and has been described as looking like an enormous wedding cake amongst other things.

As might be expected, the church has a strange and ancient tale attached to it. The story goes that on 2 May each year the churchyard is haunted by the spectre of an old man wearing a cloak. When approached by unsuspecting mortals it soon becomes clear that beneath the cloak he is nothing but a skeleton. This horrific apparition is said to be the devil himself, still searching for the soul of a man named Adam Morland who borrowed a great deal of money from him whilst unaware of his true identity. On discovering his grave error, Mr Morland then built the original church with the devil's money and upon his death on

Burgh St Peter Church has a very unusual tower and a 'haunted' churchyard.

2 May (*c.* 1101) was buried within it. On each anniversary the ghastly figure returns and has been seen many times over the centuries. A relatively recent sighting was reported by a group of boaters who came ashore to take a look at the church on 2 May 1929. They all swore that they saw the figure and that after he disappeared a 'foul, loathsome stench' remained. The eight witnesses were educated and respected people and each wrote separate accounts of their experience. Apparently they all matched!

Another local tale, albeit rather vague, tells of a ghostly wherry which sails at night on the River Waveney near Burgh St Peter Church. The captain is said to have stolen the boat and its hoard of gold. An even more obscure yarn relates to Burgh St Peter Bridge where a phantom coach has been reported, but further information is lacking.

WANDERING KNIGHTS AND DANCING MONKS

Many Norfolk churches have spooky tales connected with them but Holy Trinity Church, Ingham, near Stalham, can lay claim to one of the strangest. It centres around two monumental tombs with life-size carved effigies and goes beyond the usual ghost story. The effigy of Sir Oliver de Ingham, who founded the church

The effigy of Sir Roger de Bois rests his head on a strange 'pillow' inside Ingham Church.

and died in 1343, lies in full armour on a bed of pebbles but his tomb has been severely defaced. The tomb of Sir Roger de Bois and his wife Margaret, who passed away in 1300 and 1315 respectively, is even more remarkable. Sir Roger's effigy, also in full armour, lies next to that of his wife and rests his head on the severed head of a former adversary.

The story goes that once a year at the stroke of midnight, the effigies of the two knights miraculously come to life and rise from their tombs before walking together to Stalham Broad. There they are involved in a fight to the death with a lone opponent before returning victorious to the church and resuming their rightful positions until the next encounter. The enemy is described as a Saracen and it may be his head that Sir Roger uses as a pillow. In his *Ghosts of the Broads*, author and former Harley Street doctor Charles Sampson states that he was one of a group of four who stayed overnight in Ingham Church on 2 August (*c.* 1930)

Fragments of Ingham Priory are still attached to the church.

and actually witnessed the events unfold just as the tale describes. He and his companions allegedly followed the knights to the broad, watched them do battle, and saw them return to their tombs. It would be easy to dismiss the whole story as pure fantasy but Dr Sampson claimed that photographs taken during the vigil 'showed the empty spaces when the knights had left their tombs'. He added that movie-camera footage 'turned out, considering all things, exceedingly well'. Whether this 'evidence' was ever made public is unclear.

Another old tale tells of ghostly monks seen at the ruins of Ingham Priory, the few remaining fragments of which adjoin the church. They are said to perform a kind of dance but details are sketchy. The priory was founded in the fourteenth century and was dissolved in the 1530s. Bones were disturbed around this time, after which the dancing monks first appeared. Nineteen skeletons were discovered during repairs to the church altar in the 1860s, along with a tunnel which was not investigated. A woman's skeleton was unearthed close to the church during building work in the late twentieth century. I know of no recent reported sightings of wandering knights or dancing monks.

CATHEDRAL TALES: CONFLICT, TUNNELS AND GHOSTS

Norwich Cathedral, as with many buildings of similar age, has had a turbulent and sometimes violent history. Building work began in 1096 and a Benedictine priory existed on the site until the Dissolution in 1538. At times relations between the monks and Norwich's citizens were strained to say the least. The bloodiest episode occurred in August 1272, when a riot took place due to a dispute over a fair which the prior claimed was illegally held on priory land. The Ethelbert gate was set alight and much other damage was done. Thirty-four citizens were later hanged after being dragged through the streets of Norwich and several others were also executed.

Another riot in 1443 resulted from a dispute over the building of new grain mills which the priory objected to. Up to 3,000 citizens besieged the priory gates and issued threats against the building and its occupants. They were persuaded to disperse before major damage was done, but the Duke of Suffolk sided with the priory and the grain mills were ordered to be destroyed.

Much more damage and desecration took place in January 1644 during the English Civil War, when Oliver Cromwell's army stormed the cathedral. They destroyed numerous monuments including that of the founder, Bishop de Losinga. Many items were burned on a huge bonfire in the marketplace and the building was left without most of its doors and windows. Many priceless treasures were lost and to this day a musket ball lies embedded in the tomb of Bishop James Goldwell, who was Bishop of Norwich between 1472 and his death in 1499.

Modern visitors gaze up at the 315-foot-high (96-metre) spire – the second tallest in England after Salisbury – but probably don't think much about what may lie beneath their feet. Legend has it that several underground tunnels once existed between the cathedral and other parts of the city. It is believed that a

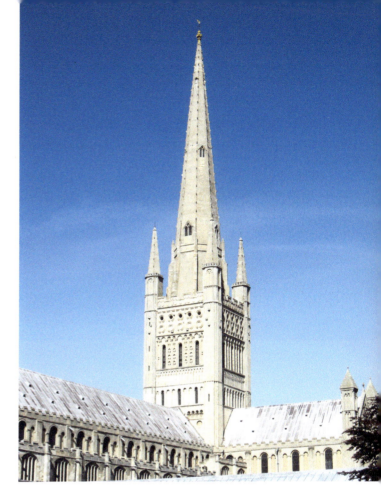

Norwich Cathedral has witnessed over 900 years of history. (Courtesy of Norwich Cathedral)

relatively short tunnel enabled monks to travel inconspicuously to and from the Maid's Head Hotel, while another linked the priory and the building perhaps best known as the former Sampson and Hercules nightclub. A longer tunnel may have led to the ancient Guildhall near the marketplace. Another claim that a tunnel once connected the cathedral and St Benet's Abbey seems very unlikely as the two sites are around 10 miles apart. A gruesome story relating to the Maid's Head tunnel alleges that some of Cromwell's soldiers tried to enter the priory by this route. They were on horseback and travelling at quite a pace when the riders and horses were decapitated by metal wires raised by Royalists hiding in the tunnel. Whether this incident actually happened is unproven, but it is claimed that the sound of thundering hooves beneath the ground can be heard in the Close at around midnight in late January.

Given its sometimes troubled past, it is perhaps surprising that tales of hauntings connected with Norwich Cathedral appear to be relatively few. Nevertheless, in his *Haunted Norwich*, author and former ghost tour guide David Chisnell mentions several strange occurrences. A female apparition enveloped in mist has been seen in the Close. She may be the wraith of a woman burned at the stake after the 1272 riot. Sir Thomas Erpingham, who was commander of Henry V's archers at the Battle of Agincourt in 1415, built the Erpingham Gate in 1420.

Left: Erpingham Gate; *right*: Statue of Sir Thomas Erpingham. (Courtesy of Norwich Cathedral)

He died in 1428 but his ghost is reputed to visit the Carnery Chapel in the Close on 25 October, the anniversary of the battle. A grotesque apparition seen at the Erpingham Gate may be a playback of the execution of Thomas Tunstall, a Catholic priest who was hanged, drawn and quartered nearby in 1616.

Another strange incident occurred as recently as 1997, following the removal of a stone staircase in the basement of a building in the Close. This appears to have stirred up poltergeist activity which took the form of loud noises and inexplicable activity in an office a few floors higher in the same building. A team of clergy specialising in unexplained phenomena was called in to investigate. The basement, which was mysteriously called the Phantom Room long before this incident, is now used for storage.

AN EGYPTIAN MUMMY AND AN AWFUL PONG!

This peculiar tale has several of the ingredients which help to make a good story: mystery, an element of slapstick comedy and a supernatural twist. It revolves around the former Priory School in Great Yarmouth, parts of which are more than 700 years old. As the name suggests, it was originally a priory before the ruins were restored and converted to a school in 1853. The events described below occurred around 1913.

A putrid stench originally thought to be caused by a dead rat was eventually traced to a case housing what was supposedly the mummy of an

The former Priory School, Great Yarmouth, with the tower of St Nicholas Minster in the background.

Egyptian princess. Why the mummy was at the school or where it came from is unknown, but its condition had deteriorated to such an extent that it needed to be removed without delay. The school backed onto the churchyard of St Nicholas' Church (now St Nicholas Minster) and the decision was made to hastily bury the mummy there at midnight, apparently in deference to ancient Egyptian custom. When this had been carried out the case was returned to the school and for a while the atmosphere in the building was much more pleasant. Several weeks later the pong returned and was found to be coming from the 'empty' case. On further examination it was revealed that part of a leg remained inside and was the source of the odour. This was duly buried with the rest of the mummy and the smell never returned.

The supernatural twist alluded to earlier is that between the two interments unexplained knocking was heard on the front door of the vicarage and from inside the church. The vicar's sleep was interrupted on several nights but on each occasion he found nobody outside. The church was searched after workmen heard noises coming from within but it was found to be empty. As word got around the town, a large crowd gathered at the churchyard and police had to cordon it off. After the princess's leg was reunited with the rest of her body, the knocking ceased. It was obviously suspected that the noises were made by hoaxers but nobody was caught and the whole thing remains a mystery. Some, of course, were convinced that the offended Egyptian princess was responsible for the cacophony due to her leg being left behind during the botched first burial!

MYSTERIOUS HAPPENINGS IN SNETTISHAM

This intriguing tale is believed by some to offer compelling evidence of death survival, though ultimately it poses as many questions as it answers.

A lady named Mrs Goodeve was staying with friends in Clifton when she claimed that in the early hours of 9 October 1893, she was visited by the ghost of a woman. The following night she was awoken again by the same spirit, accompanied this time by a male figure who gave his name as Henry Barnard and stated that he was buried in Snettisham churchyard in Norfolk. He gave Mrs Goodeve the dates of his marriage and death plus other information and instructed her to go there and check the dates in the church registers. If she found them to be accurate, she should return at 1.15 a.m. on the following day and wait beside the grave of Robert Cobb inside the church. A third apparition then appeared; a man who seemed to be consumed by sorrow

Snettisham Church, where a strange nocturnal vigil took place in 1893.

whose identity she was not at liberty to divulge. The female figure did not disclose her name but gave the date of her marriage. Mrs Goodeve's description of the woman matched that of a Mrs Seagrim, who died in the house at Clifton on 22 December 1878. Her daughter confirmed that the date given, 26 September 1860, was correct.

Mrs Goodeve, who seems to have been receptive to communications from the spirit world, was not unduly fazed by the visitations and was determined to visit Snettisham – a place she had never heard of – to check for herself. On arrival she examined the registers and found the dates given by Henry Barnard's ghost to be correct. Gaining access to the church during the night proved to be more difficult, but she managed to persuade the parish clerk, John Bishop, to unlock the building. After checking for intruders, he then locked her in the church alone before returning around twenty-five minutes later. Following her vigil, during which she claimed to have encountered the spirit of a tall man, she stayed overnight at the home of John Bishop and his wife, whose six-year-old son Percival had drowned in 1886. Before leaving Clifton, Mrs Goodeve revealed to her friends that Henry Barnard's spirit had passed this information to her. The next day she visited Barnard's daughter at nearby Cobb Hall and passed on a personal message from her father along with roses from his grave as instructed. Mrs Bishop may also have known the secret but all three women went to their graves without revealing it.

Against Mrs Goodeve's wishes the story was leaked to the press and later appeared in a book published by the Psychic Press. Robert Cobb, whose grave Mrs Goodeve waited beside, owned Cobb Hall until his death in 1743. It was rumoured that Henry Barnard may have acquired the property in dubious circumstances and that this could have been a trigger for unrest beyond the grave. Mrs Seagrim, whose spirit seems to have acted as a celestial go-between, appears to have been a member of the Cobb family.

THE MADDERMARKET 'MONK'

Many theatres are believed to be haunted, including the small Maddermarket Theatre in St John's Alley, Norwich. During medieval times the plant madder was traded at a market on the site, hence the unusual name. The plant's roots were valued as a source of dye used in the wool trade. A converted Roman Catholic chapel originally constructed in 1794, the Maddermarket Theatre was opened by Nugent Monck in 1921. Since then the theatre has had a reputation as a place of unexplained happenings.

Usually described as either a priest or a monk, a mysterious figure was first seen by the owner not long after the theatre opened. Audience members have witnessed it standing alongside the stage and actors have seen it at the rear of the auditorium during a performance. A young actress was said to have been nudged to one side out of the path of a falling light, and an actor reported being hugged by unseen arms after becoming agitated when he forgot his lines. It was also

The Maddermarket Theatre, Norwich.

claimed that a group of schoolchildren spoke of seeing a monk after attending a performance at the theatre. No such character was portrayed onstage that day and their teachers did not see the figure. Reliable dates of recorded sightings are sketchy but most seem to go back several decades.

Norfolk's Phantom Ladies

Following on from the previous chapter, Norfolk has a host of phantom ladies who are variously described as being pale, shadowy, grey, white or brown in appearance. Below I relate a few of the old tales of female spectres that have been handed down the centuries and still have the power to send shudders down the spine.

QUEEN ANNE BOLEYN

Anne Boleyn, the second wife of King Henry VIII, was executed on 19 May 1536. Since then, her many alleged supernatural activities have ensured her reputation as 'the most restless of the royal dead' and 'the hardest-working ghost in England!' Spectral sightings have been reported at several Norfolk locations including Blickling Hall, Salle Church and Caister Castle, as well as the Tower of London, Hever Castle, Hampton Court Palace and Marwell Hall.

Anne Boleyn's ill-fated marriage to the volatile Tudor monarch and subsequent events leading to a violent demise are well documented. A legend still endures that after her beheading at the Tower of London Anne's body was moved under cover of darkness and secretly buried at midnight inside Salle Church in Norfolk, where some of her ancestors were interred. A few select mourners were said to have attended the nocturnal funeral service. During the long journey from London to North Norfolk her body supposedly found a temporary safe haven in an Essex church. Charles Dickens incorporated the Salle Church legend into his fictional 1848 work *Bentley's Miscellany*. In her *Life of Anne Boleyn (Vol. 4)*, historical author Agnes Strickland also mentions the tale, as does Francis Lancelott in his 1858 book *The Queens of England*. It is rumoured that the anonymous black slab thought to mark her burial place was once raised but nothing was found underneath, though whether this actually happened is unclear.

The official version of events is that Anne Boleyn was buried in the chapel of St Peter ad Vincula at the Tower of London and there she remains to this day, though possibly without her severed head, which may have been tossed into the murky Thames. An elm chest believed to contain her body was discovered during renovations to the chapel in the 1870s. Another legend states that Anne requested that her heart should be removed and buried at St Mary's Church, Erwarton, Suffolk, and that her wishes were carried out by an uncle. A heart-shaped lead casket was found there in the 1830s and reburied.

According to legend, Anne Boleyn *may* have been buried in Salle Church.

Blickling Hall near Aylsham in North Norfolk may have been Anne Boleyn's birthplace, though Hever Castle in Kent stakes a similar claim. She was born between 1501 and 1507 and probably lived for at least a short while at the original Blickling Hall, later replaced by the present Jacobean house which is haunted by several ghosts. On the anniversary of her execution the former queen arrived at Blickling Hall at midnight after dashing around the Aylsham area in a black coach. Given the manner of her death it is unsurprising that she cradles her severed head in her lap, while her torso glows red and lights up the dark coach. Less logically, the coachman and horses are also headless. At journey's end she leaves her carriage and floats into the house. Similar tales claim that the ghosts of Anne's father and brother are also seen in headless form on the night of 19 May. In retribution for betraying his daughter, Sir Thomas Boleyn – who in life actually managed to retain his head – is condemned to travel at high speed over twelve bridges between Wroxham and Blickling in a carriage pursued by screaming demons.

THE MYSTERY OF WHITE WOMAN LANE

Just to the north of Norwich there is a road mysteriously named White Woman Lane. According to local folklore a young lady married the Lord of Catton Old Hall during the reign of Elizabeth I. The couple's wedding took place at the church of St Mary and St Margaret in Church Lane, Sprowston. On her wedding day the bride died in peculiar circumstances under the hooves of her new husband's horse, but whether it was a tragic accident or a heinous act of murder is unknown.

Catton Old Hall is linked with the legend of White Woman Lane.

Other versions of the tale state that the lady was the daughter of the Lord of the Manor and had a relationship either with her father's coachman or a son of the coachman. He lived a short distance from the hall, possibly on what is now White Woman Lane, and she would secretly leave the hall for nocturnal meetings with him. These variations have similar endings, but with the bride being run over either just before or soon after her wedding by a horse and coach driven by her betrothed.

Whether she was the lord's wife or his daughter, her ghost is said to walk in her white wedding dress from the Old Hall on Lodge Lane, Old Catton, along the road now named in her memory, through the grounds of Oak Lodge Farm to Sprowston parish church. She has reportedly been seen many times over the centuries, though I have not heard of any recent sightings. Once a quiet rural area, White Woman Lane and Lodge Lane are now busy thoroughfares and have become heavily urbanised. These changes may have curtailed the unfortunate lady's restless wanderings, but only time will tell.

THE WHITE LADY OF WORSTEAD CHURCH

The story goes that on Christmas Eve 1830, a local man had a fatal encounter with the White Lady of Worstead Church in North Norfolk. He and several other men had spent the evening drinking at the King's Head public house close by.

A mysterious White Lady is said to haunt Worstead Church.

They were all aware of the old tale that the White Lady materialised in the church tower at midnight on 24 December, but one of the revellers insisted on climbing into the belfry alone to ring the bell. He said that if he saw the White Lady he would kiss her. After hearing nothing his friends reluctantly followed him into the tower and found him crouched there in a terrible state. They carried the man back to the pub but he died soon afterwards. It is said that his last coherent words were, 'I've seen her, I've seen her!'

Despite this story, it is believed that the White Lady is a benevolent spirit usually associated with healing rather than scaring people to death. Her identity is unknown but her wanderings are apparently not limited to the belfry. An intriguing photograph taken in 1975 appears to show a glowing figure wearing a bonnet, sitting behind a woman who visited the church with her husband and son. Mrs Diane Berthelot was photographed by her husband Peter as she quietly prayed for relief from health problems. The apparition was not seen at the time but appeared when the photograph was developed. The couple later returned to Norfolk from their home in Essex and showed the image to the late Revd Pettit, at that time the vicar of Worstead. He was aware of the legend and informed them that the White Lady was known locally as a healer.

In 2011, Mr and Mrs Berthelot presented a copy of the photograph to the new owner of the former King's Head, now renamed The White Lady in honour of the phantom. It was reported in the local press that after the name was changed the new owner experienced unexplained happenings in the pub. When I visited in 2018, the framed picture was on the wall but the person on duty was unaware of any unusual occurrences in the building.

THE GREY LADY OF TOMBLAND ALLEY

The tale behind the Grey Lady of Tombland Alley in Norwich is a sad and grisly one. Despite its eerie name, Tombland just means 'open space' but the area has an eventful and sometimes violent history. On one side of Tombland is the mighty Anglican cathedral; on the opposite side stand a variety of buildings including the historic Augustine Steward House, named after a former mayor of Norwich. An opening beneath the upper stories of the house leads to Tombland Alley, a narrow shortcut between Tombland and Princes Street. The building housed soldiers of the royal armies sent to crush Kett's Rebellion in 1549 (*see* 'Other Assorted Tales'). The ill-fated Lord Sheffield spent his last night there before being mortally wounded in battle the next day.

Later that century, Norwich was in the deadly grip of the plague which took the lives of thousands of its citizens. The policy at the time was to try to prevent the spread of disease by sealing up plague houses when all occupants were thought to have succumbed to the inevitable. Augustine Steward House was sealed up for several weeks in 1578, but when it was reopened, and the dreadful job of removing the decaying bodies of the family began, the full horror was revealed. It is claimed that human flesh was found in the mouth and throat of

Above left: A Grey Lady has been seen in Tombland Alley, Norwich.

Above right: Entrance to Tombland Alley beneath Augustine Steward House.

one of the daughters and tooth marks were visible on the legs of both of her parents. The awful truth seemed to be that the girl was the only one of her family still alive when the house was sealed and that she had resorted to cannibalism in a desperate but futile attempt to survive.

Since then a female figure dressed in grey has been seen in Tombland Alley, Augustine Steward House and the former Sampson and Hercules nightclub next door. Several reported sightings took place between the early 1970s and around the turn of the century. It is claimed that quite recently she was seen to enter St George's Church by the front door before passing through locked doors at the rear leading to Tombland Alley.

RAYNHAM HALL'S BROWN LADY

Raynham Hall in North Norfolk is well known for its ghostly Brown Lady. She is said to be the restless spirit of Dorothy Walpole – a sister of Britain's first Prime Minister, Sir Robert Walpole – who died in mysterious circumstances on 29 March 1726, aged around forty. The cause of death was recorded as smallpox, but rumours soon circulated that she fell – or was pushed – down the hall's main staircase and broke her neck. The finger of suspicion was pointed at her jealous second husband Charles Townshend, who allegedly separated Dorothy from her children and locked her in her bedroom.

Many have reportedly encountered the Brown Lady, including the future King George IV when he was Prince of Wales. He claimed to have seen the figure of 'a little lady all dressed in brown' and left the hall almost immediately, vowing never to return. In a separate incident, Captain Frederick Marryat, an author and friend of Charles Dickens, fired his gun at the spectre which was carrying a lighted lamp. The sighting was witnessed by two other guests and the bullet was found embedded in a door panel. The phantom was also seen by Lady Townshend and her son in 1926.

A very famous but highly controversial photograph of the alleged ghost was first published in *Country Life* magazine in December 1936, and a cropped version is reproduced here. The photograph was taken at around 4 p.m. on 19 September 1936 by Captain Hubert Provand, when his assistant, Indrie Shira, claimed to have seen a vague form on the grand staircase. Provand himself saw nothing at the time. The picture has since been described as everything from 'the best-ever ghost photograph' to a blatant fraud. Many consider the image to be a double exposure and some have suggested that the mysterious figure may be a model of the Virgin Mary superimposed over an empty staircase. The negative and camera were examined at the time but no evidence of deliberate deceit was found. Over eighty years later nothing has been proved and the jury is still out.

The Raynham Hall 'ghost'
photograph. (Provand, 1936)

Traditional Folk Tales

THE SWAFFHAM PEDLAR

A rather convoluted old tale relates to a pedlar named John Chapman of Swaffham, who dreamt on several consecutive nights that he should visit London where he would receive fortuitous news. He finally set out for the capital with his dog and headed for London Bridge as the dreams had instructed. After standing on the bridge for much of the day the pedlar was approached by a curious shopkeeper. Chapman told the man the reason for his visit but was met with derision. The shopkeeper informed him that he also had preposterous dreams but

The Swaffham Pedlar as depicted in Swaffham Church (left) and on the town sign (right).

was not gullible enough to give them any credence. His dreams had instructed him to go to a place he'd never heard of called Swaffham and seek out the residence of a local pedlar. There he should dig beneath an apple tree in his garden where a pot of gold was awaiting discovery.

Without revealing his identity the pedlar and his dog returned to Norfolk as fast as their sore feet would carry them. Once home, Chapman dug beneath the tree and to his amazement and joy did indeed locate the pot of gold the mocking shopkeeper had spoken of. The pot carried a mysterious inscription in Latin, later translated by a passing monk or wise man as, 'Under me doth lie, Another richer far than I.'

The pedlar waited until nightfall before again digging under his apple tree and eventually, much deeper in the earth than before, he came upon a second pot far larger than the first. On opening the pot he found it too was brimming with gold. Not wishing to draw attention to his new-found wealth, Chapman told nobody and continued to live frugally for some time before finally donating at least some of his riches to the local church which was in need of urgent repair. This amazed and perplexed the other parishioners who had no idea that the seemingly poor pedlar in their midst was in reality a very rich man.

This story sounds fanciful but official records confirm that after becoming Churchwarden in 1462, John Chapman paid for the rebuilding of the church tower and north aisle, which must have been an enormous outlay. Carved figures of the Swaffham Pedlar and his trusty dog can be found inside the church and they are also immortalised on the town sign.

THE BABES IN THE WOOD

First published as a ballad in 1595 but now best known as a popular pantomime, the tale of the Babes in the Wood has long been absorbed into Norfolk folklore. The basic story is that two young children, a boy and a girl, were orphaned and placed in the care of their uncle. The boy, traditionally called Edgar Truelove, was around three years old and was set to inherit the then enormous sum of £300 a year upon turning twenty-one. His younger sister Jane would have received a lump sum if she had married. If neither child reached adulthood all of the money would go to their uncle.

After living with their uncle and aunt for around a year, the youngsters' fate was about to be sealed. Although his wife doted on the siblings their uncle was growing tired of them. He hatched a plot to get his hands on their inheritance and told his wife he was sending them to be raised by friends in London. He then secretly paid two men to murder them in Wayland Wood near Watton. As they were leading the children into the wood, a fight broke out between the two men and one was killed. The other continued to take his captives deep into the heart of the wood and told them to remain there till he returned with food. They obeyed but he never went back and the Babes perished from hunger. According to the tale the children's uncle died in debtor's prison while the villain who abandoned them

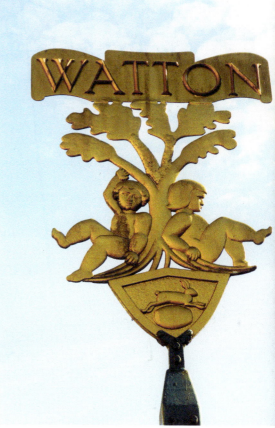

The Babes in the Wood are featured on the Griston village sign (left) and Watton town sign (right).

in the wood was later hanged. He was caught and sentenced for an unrelated crime but made a confession before his death.

Wayland Wood was much larger in the sixteenth century than it is today and the Babes are said to have breathed their last beneath an enormous oak tree which was struck by lightning in 1879. The tale appears to be a romanticised version of actual events that took place during the 1560s. Seven-year-old Thomas de Grey became an orphan when his father died. If he reached majority he would inherit his father's estate but in the case of his early death it would go to his uncle Robert de Grey. At the age of eleven, Thomas died in suspicious circumstances while or just after visiting his stepmother at Baconsthorpe in North Norfolk. Robert de Grey, of Griston Hall near Watton, has long been associated with the 'wicked uncle' of the Babes in the Wood story, though whether there is any justification for this remains uncertain. He was later imprisoned for being a Roman Catholic but passed away at Merton Hall and is said to have owed a considerable sum of money in unpaid fines.

Wayland Wood, the traditional location of the Babes in the Wood legend.

Curiously, his ill-fated nephew Thomas had already 'married' a young girl named Elizabeth Drury, who survived to adulthood and later had children.

The Babes are featured in very different ways on Watton town sign and Griston village sign. Despite there being no clear evidence of children being abandoned in Wayland Wood – also known locally as Wailing Wood – the legend lives on and it is said that their cries can still be heard if you venture there at night.

THE LEGEND OF TOM HICKATHRIFT

This very old tale is set on the borders of Norfolk and Cambridgeshire and possibly dates back to shortly before the Norman Conquest. Tom Hickathrift, the hero of the piece, grew remarkably tall with muscles to match. One account says that at the age of ten he was already '8 feet (2.44 metres) tall and 5 feet (1.52 metres) in thickness', with 'hands like shoulders of mutton'. Tom was lazy and had an enormous appetite for food and drink, much to the horror of his poor widowed mother who was struggling to make ends meet. He later found a job carting beer and was said to posses the strength of twenty ordinary men. On his way home one day he followed a shortcut across the land of the notorious and much-feared Wisbech Giant, an enormous cave-dwelling ogre much larger even than Tom. Armed with a huge club, the angry ogre went on the attack but Hickathrift ripped the axle and a wheel from his cart and bravely fought his adversary. Despite his size advantage the lumbering ogre was vanquished and a triumphant Tom was hailed a hero by the grateful locals. After slaying the ogre, Tom took his land and treasure. Now a rich man, his fame grew and he was summoned to the court of the king to be knighted.

Tom Hickathrift's grave, Tilney All Saints churchyard. (Photo: N. Stockman)

Another tale about Hickathrift involves a challenge he laid down at his local public house to any man who could defeat him at any sport or activity. A tiny tinker claimed he could beat the mighty Sir Tom at 'broom dancing' and proceeded to put on a dazzling display. When handed the broom and asked to duplicate the tinker's intricate moves, Hickathrift failed miserably and declared his diminutive opponent a worthy winner. In his later years he hurled a huge stone to decide where he should be buried. After ricocheting off Tilney All Saints Church it came to rest a short distance away. Upon his death, Tom was duly buried at the spot. A grave measuring 7 feet 6 inches (2.28 metres) in length and supposedly containing his bones can still be seen in the churchyard.

How much, if any, of the legend of Tom Hickathrift is based on fact is impossible to say. Comparisons have been drawn with a local landowner by the name of Hickafric, who apparently armed himself with a cart axle and wheel and threatened anyone who trespassed on his property, and a twelfth-century knight called Frederick de Tilney. The latter took part in the crusades and was said to be very tall and strong. Perhaps between them these two individuals may have at least contributed to the story.

TALES OF SAINT WITHBURGA

Little historical information is known about the woman known as St Withburga or Wihtburh, apart from legends passed down through the centuries. Traditionally she was claimed to be the youngest daughter of King Anna of the East Angles, though some historians dispute this. Her date of birth is unknown but she is said to have founded a church and convent at Dereham in 654 and died there on 17 March 743. Assuming these dates are accurate, Withburga would have been an extremely old woman when she died.

After she prayed for food a pair of wild does appeared by a stream and allowed her nuns to milk them each morning. The milk was a valuable addition to their diet and was used to make butter and cheese. Some regarded this unusual occurrence as a miracle and Withburga soon became popular in the village. This angered the local reeve, who resented the attention she was receiving from the locals. He set out with his dogs to hunt down the deer but fell from his horse and was killed.

Upon her death, Withburga's body was buried in the churchyard and remained there for fifty-five years before being exhumed. It was claimed to be in perfect condition with no sign of decomposition, which was again hailed as a miracle. She was then reburied in a tomb inside her own church. The convent was torn down in 870 by invading Danes, but the saint's tomb was spared and continued to be a place of pilgrimage before her mortal remains were disturbed again in 974. This time her body was stolen from the tomb one night and taken to Ely Abbey. There it was quickly reinterred close to the remains of three other women supposed to be her sisters. Men from Dereham gave chase when they discovered what had happened and some accounts speak of a fierce battle between the two sides.

St Withburga's Well, East Dereham churchyard.

They were unable to prevent the theft of their saint but on returning to the empty tomb found a spring of water where the body had been.

The theft of Withburga's body was intended to raise Ely's standing as a place of pilgrimage, though inadvertently the holy well greatly increased the number of pilgrims visiting Dereham. The spring was believed to have healing properties and for hundreds of years people drank the water and prayed there. The well was refurbished in the mid-twentieth century and is located in the churchyard of the present St Nicholas' Church in the town centre. Saint Withburga's remains were lost when Ely Abbey was destroyed during the Reformation.

HERE BE DRAGONS!

For centuries the dragon was believed to be a real fire-breathing beast and it became part of Norfolk's folklore. The legend of the Ludham Dragon is one of many local tales recorded by historian and author W. H. Cooke.

A large dragon once lived in a burrow close to St Catherine's Church, Ludham. The beast 'had wings and was covered with scales' and 'measured 12–15 feet (3.6–4.5 metres) in length'. It terrorised the community and local folk lived in fear of the dragon. After several unsuccessful attempts, its burrow was finally

The Ludham Dragon
as depicted in Ludham
Church.

blocked by 'a single large flint stone' rolled in by 'a courageous local parishioner'
while the dragon was out sunbathing. On returning to its lair and being unable to
gain entry, it flew off towards St Benet's Abbey and angrily crashed into the walls,
knocking them to the ground. The Ludham Dragon was never seen again.

Author Frank Meeres retells this tale in his *Paranormal Norfolk* (Amberley
Publishing, 2010) and also mentions a documented case recorded in an issue of the
Norfolk Chronicle dated 28 September 1782. A snake measuring 5 feet 8 inches
(1.7 metres) long and with a circumference of nearly 3 feet (0.9 metres)
was killed in Ludham by a local man named Jasper Andrews. Could this have
been the true event behind the legend or does the Ludham Dragon go back
further in time? Interestingly, the creature is sometimes called the Ludham Worm,
which makes it seem rather less scary. A carving of the dragon can be seen inside
Ludham Church.

The city of Norwich has a rich tradition of snapdragons, used for centuries
in street processions. Snapdragons of various sizes and designs were operated
by entertainers on St George's Day and featured a mechanical snapping jaw.
The tradition began in the late fourteenth century when the Norwich Guild
of St George was founded and continued until around the early nineteenth
century. Snapdragons returned to the streets of Norwich in the 1980s as part
of the annual Lord Mayor's Procession. Ancient snapdragons can be seen in
Norwich Castle Museum and an impressive modern replica is on display in
St George's Church, Tombland.

A crouching dragon is carved in stone on one side of the archway of Norwich
Cathedral's Ethelbert Gate, ready to pounce on a man (presumably St George)

Above: A reproduction Snapdragon, St George's Church, Norwich.

Left: A crouching dragon on Norwich Cathedral's Ethelbert Gate. (Courtesy of Norwich Cathedral)

on the opposite side who is armed with a sword and shield. Also in Norwich, the historic Dragon Hall in King Street appropriately has dragons on a sign outside and an ancient carving of one inside. Dragons of a different kind briefly appeared in Norwich during the summer of 2015, when beautifully painted sculptures were placed across the city to form the 'GoGoDragons!' trail.

WILL KEMP'S 'NINE DAIES WONDER'

One of the greatest comedy events or publicity stunts of the first Elizabethan age was undertaken by William Kemp (or Kempe), an actor, clown and dancer who worked with William Shakespeare. According to various accounts, Kemp morris danced over a hundred miles from London to Norwich, the two largest cities in England at that time, in just nine days during 1599 or 1600.

After dancing through Essex, Suffolk and into Norfolk, Will Kemp eventually arrived in Norwich and was greeted by great crowds eager to witness such a spectacle. Along the way he handed out brightly coloured garters to people he met.

Will Kemp's plaque in St John's Alley, Norwich.

His journey ended at St John's Alley, where he jumped over the churchyard wall of St John Maddermarket. He then pinned his buskins (boots) to the door of Norwich Guildhall. Kemp was accompanied on his quest by musician Thomas Slye, who played the pipe and drum, timekeeper George Spratt, and a servant called William Bee.

Kemp wrote of his exploits in his *Nine Daies Wonder* published in 1600. Although the dancing was apparently completed in nine days, he actually arrived in Norwich twenty-three days after setting out from the capital. The rest of the time was spent recuperating and sheltering from the weather at various places along the route. Heavy snow hindered his progress for a while before he was taken into the centre of Norwich on horseback and given a hero's welcome. A few days later he re-entered the city on foot to finally complete his journey.

Will Kemp was born *c.* 1560 and joined Lord Strange's Men, an acting troupe, around 1592. He later became an original member of the Chamberlain's Men alongside William Shakespeare, Richard Burbage and others. During this time Kemp played the part of Dogberry in *Much Ado About Nothing* and Peter in *Romeo and Juliet*. He probably also performed as Bottom in *A Midsummer Night's Dream*, Lancelot Gobbo in *The Merchant of Venice*, and Falstaff.

A woodcarving of Will Kemp in Chapelfield Gardens, Norwich.

Kemp left the Chamberlain's Men in 1599, seemingly due to what would now be called 'artistic differences'. He frequently strayed from his script and incorporated bawdy humour and risqué jigs into his roles. This may have annoyed the Bard and other members of the troupe and led to his departure. It has been speculated that Kemp's journey to Norwich may have been a parting shot at his former colleagues to prove that he was a star in his own right. The stunt probably generated much-needed income after losing his regular employment. Kemp, who is also said to have rowed the entire length of the River Thames in a paper boat, embarked on an acting tour of Europe in 1601 and reportedly morris danced through Germany and Italy. He later briefly joined the Earl of Worcester's Men on his return to England and is thought to have died from the plague in London around 1603.

In Norwich, a plaque in St John's Alley and a walkway named Will Kemp Way (at the back of the Forum) keep his name alive. A woodcarving in Chapelfield Gardens also records the visit of Kemp and his companions over 400 years ago.

A HOLY RELIC AND A LOVELORN MONK

Bromholm Priory at Bacton on the North Norfolk coast was founded by William de Glanville, Lord of Bacton, in 1113 as a small priory for cluniac monks. Two old tales have endured which give a glimpse of monastic life there hundreds of years ago.

Bromholm Priory was once a place of pilgrimage due to a claim that it possessed fragments of the cross on which Jesus Christ was crucified. This and other relics including two of St Margaret's fingers were stolen after the death of Baldwin, Emperor of Constantinople, in 1206. The hoard, which also included jewels, was brought to England by a chaplain to Baldwin known only as Hugh. He then spent several years touring the country and selling off parts of his booty to various religious houses before arriving at the isolated and impoverished Bromholm Priory in 1223. The much-travelled Hugh is said to have been a Norfolk man and wished to end his days in the county. The abbot agreed to allow him and his two sons to join the community at Bromholm in exchange for the pieces of the True Cross. On its arrival in North Norfolk, the holy relic soon put Bromholm on the pilgrimage map. It gained a reputation as a place where the sick were healed and even raised from the dead. No less than thirty-nine people were claimed to have been resurrected and nineteen more cured of blindness after touching the relic. Bromholm became rich through donations from pilgrims and the original wooden priory was rebuilt in stone. Two Kings – Henry III and Edward II – also visited the remote location. Chaucer wrote of 'the holy cross of Bromeholme' in *The Reeves Tale* and William Langland mentioned 'the Roode of Bromholm' in his *Vision of Piers Plowman*.

All this wealth and fame is said to have ended abruptly in 1424 when Hugh Pie, the chaplain of Ludney, allegedly threw the relic into a fire. He denied the claim and an alternative version suggests that he destroyed a picture of the cross

The ruined gatehouse of Bromholm Priory, Bacton.

rather than the actual article. There is a written record that it still existed in February 1537, when the priory was dissolved.

The other story relating to Bromholm Priory tells of a young monk named Hubert de Coalville, who discovered a young lady lying on the beach at Bacton during a storm. She had been washed ashore from a ship that had sunk in view of a large crowd including a number of monks. Hubert took her back to the priory, where she recovered – at least for a short while. Her name was Edith and she and Hubert fell in love with each other. They enjoyed walks along the seashore together but the young monk's vocation meant that nothing could come of their romantic yearnings. Hubert was left broken-hearted when Edith died and he appears to have passed away soon after, though we are not told how much time elapsed between their first meeting and poor Edith's death or how long the young monk survived his heartbreak. Hubert and Edith were buried next to each other 'by the willows that oershade the streamlet by the woodland hill'. It is said that Hubert's restless spirit once haunted the abbey and that the wraiths of the unlucky couple were seen on the beach together. However, no modern sightings seem to have been reported, so time may have curtailed their wanderings. The priory ruins are not open to the public, though what remains of the gatehouse is situated close to the coast road.

A GREAT OAK FROM A WITCH'S WOODEN LEG!

One of Norfolk's most mysterious and enigmatic ruins can be found in woodland off Back Lane, East Somerton, near Winterton-on-Sea, though it is so well camouflaged that it is easy to miss. The most intriguing feature of the ruined Church of St Mary is a large oak tree growing in the centre of the nave and rising through what was once the roof.

According to an old tale, a local witch was buried beneath the nave – possibly while still alive – and that from her wooden leg the now mighty oak grew. She put a curse on the church and as it developed the tree demolished the building, giving the witch posthumous revenge. Some claim that she still appears if a visitor is foolish enough to walk around the tree three times. Luckily, I hadn't heard that part of the story when I visited, so wasn't tempted to find out. Dear reader, you have been warned…

Whether any aspect of the legend of the Witch of East Somerton and her wooden leg is based on fact is lost in the mists of time, but the ruined church is a strange and fascinating place to visit. It appears to have been built in the fifteenth century before being abandoned around 200 years later.

Did this tree in the ruined East Somerton Church sprout from a witch's wooden leg?

Tales from the Coast

The Norfolk coast has spawned all kinds of tales relating to smuggling, shipwrecks, lost villages and even mermaids. This chapter looks at assorted stories from around the county, starting in the ancient port of Great Yarmouth.

NORFOLK'S ALTERNATIVE NELSON'S COLUMN

Horatio, Lord Nelson (1758–1805) is often described as Norfolk's favourite son and his life story has been told innumerable times in the years since his death at the Battle of Trafalgar. It is less well known that a pillar commemorating the naval hero was erected in his home county two decades before the much more famous Nelson's Column in Trafalgar Square, London. Officially named the Norfolk Naval Pillar but also known locally as Nelson's Monument and the Britannia Monument, it is located just off the seafront in Great Yarmouth.

The monument has intrigued and mystified natives and visitors alike and various stories have circulated around the town over the last two centuries. It is often asked why a tribute to Nelson should be topped by a figure of Britannia rather than the great man himself – and why, when Britannia is said to rule the waves, does she face inland rather than out to sea? The huge figure was a late amendment by Yarmouth Corporation to William Wilkins' original design, which specified a representation of a ship at the top of the pillar. Although there appears to be no official record of why she faces inland, it is thought that Britannia is either looking towards the harbour or, much more distant, Nelson's birthplace of Burnham Thorpe in North Norfolk.

A tale handed down through successive generations claimed that the person responsible committed suicide by leaping from the top of the monument, when he realised that Britannia faced the 'wrong' way. This story is probably a distortion of two tragedies that definitely occurred there in the nineteenth century. The first involved the surveyor Thomas Sutton, who died from a heart attack after climbing to the top shortly before the monument opened to the public. His gravestone at St Nicholas Minster records that he passed away 'on the summit' of the pillar on 1 June 1819, aged sixty-five. The second took place in 1863, when an acrobat named Charles Marsh was entertaining a large crowd with increasingly dangerous tricks before falling to his death from Britannia's shoulders. These two events may have become intertwined in the town's folklore, though it seems more likely that the later one – which was probably witnessed by thousands of

The giant figure of Britannia atop the Norfolk Naval Pillar, Great Yarmouth.

people and must have caused quite a stir at the time – simply became confused when retold numerous times over the generations.

Until his death aged eighty-two in 1867, the monument's first custodian was James Sharman, who took part in the Battle of Trafalgar aboard the *Victory* and often said that he was one of the men who helped take the dying Nelson below deck after he was shot. Among those who visited the pillar during Sharman's time were Charles Dickens – who based the character of Ham Peggotty in his novel *David Copperfield* on him – and Nelson's daughter Horatia.

The original Coade stone figures of Britannia and six caryatids beneath her were superseded by concrete replicas in 1896 and finally by reinforced plastic versions in 1982. The monument underwent restoration before the bicentenary of Nelson's death in 2005.

THE GREAT YARMOUTH SUSPENSION BRIDGE DISASTER

An excited crowd several thousand strong lined the banks of the River Bure in Great Yarmouth on 2 May 1845. Many were children and despite heavy rain they were looking forward to seeing a clown named Nelson sail past in a washtub drawn by four geese. The stunt was planned for around 5 p.m. and was intended to promote Cooke's Equestrian Circus, which was in town at the time.

Several hundred people were gathered on a suspension bridge over the river to watch the clown and geese pass underneath. As the spectators moved from one side to the other, the bridge partly collapsed under the strain and many of them fell into the water. Tragically, fifty-nine of the seventy-eight fatalities were children, most of them aged between five and thirteen years. The youngest were Charles Dye and Mary Ann Lake, who were both just two years old. The oldest person to die was sixty-four-year-old Mary Ann Ditcham. Many more were injured but were saved from drowning or freed from the wreckage of the bridge. The bridge's span had been increased from the original 63 feet (19.2 metres) to 86 feet (26.2 metres), and this change was believed to have contributed to the tragedy. The quality of some of the welding and iron used was found to be substandard.

The disaster, which is said to have claimed more lives than any other single recorded event in Great Yarmouth's history, is commemorated by a large granite memorial close to the spot where the bridge stood. Taking the form of an open

The Great Yarmouth suspension bridge disaster memorial.

THE GREAT YARMOUTH SUSPENSION BRIDGE DISASTER
2nd May 1845
To commemorate the 78 people who lost their lives of which 59 were young children, while watching a clown named 'NELSON' being pulled up the River Bure in a wash tub by four real geese.

Name	Age	Name	Age
ROBERT ADAMS	aged 7 years	SARAH JOHNSON	aged 14 years
CAROLINE AUGER	aged 10 years	THOMAS JOHNSON	aged 8 years
HARRIET BUSSEY	aged 26 years	MARY ANN JENKERSON	aged 10 years
GEORGE JOHN HENRY		MAUD JUNIPER	aged 9 years
BELOE	aged 9 years	MARY ANN KING	aged 11 years
SARAH ANN BUTTIFANT	aged 18 years	FREDERICK LUCAS	aged 62 years
EMILY H. BORKING	aged 5 years	MARY ANN LAKE	aged 2 years
BENJAMIN PATTERSON		WILLIAM LYONS	aged 6 years
BURTON	aged 7 years	HARRIET MARY LITTLE	aged 12 years
CHRISTOPHER BARBER	aged 11 years	JOSEPH LIVINGSTONE	aged 6 years
ISSAC BRADBERRY	aged 20 years	MATILDA LIVINGSTONE	aged 7 years
ANN BECKET	aged 8 years	CLARA MAY	aged 20 years
JAMES SEAMAN BUCK	aged 4 years	SUSAN MEARS	aged 8 years
REEDER THURSTON BALLS	aged 16 years	ELIZABETH MANSHIP	aged 28 years
JAMES CHURCH	aged 7 years	ELIZABETH MORGAN	aged 62 years
CAROLINE CHURCH	aged 16 years	ROBERT MAZE	aged 26 years
ELIZA CROWE	aged 13 years	ELIZABETH POWLEY	aged 20 years
ELIZABETH CONYERS	aged 13 years	RICHARD POWLEY	aged 4 years
JANE COLE	aged 16 years	AMELIA POWLEY	aged 10 years
WILLIAM DURRANT	aged 12 years	CHARLOTTE PARKER	aged 8 years
MARY ANN DITCHAM	aged 64 years	PHEOBE ANN RICHARDSON	aged 17 years
ELIZA DUFFIELD	aged 10 years	LYDIA ROBERTS	aged 12 years
BENJAMIN DYE	aged 9 years	MARY ANN ROBERTS	aged 19 years
CHARLES DYE	aged 2 years	ELIZABETH READ	aged 6 years
MARIA EDWARDS	aged 12 years	ANN MARIA SCOTTEN	aged 20 years
DAVID EBBAGE	aged 9 years	MARIA STOLWORTHY	aged 14 years
HANNAH FIELD	aged 12 years	HARRIET TANN	aged 15 years
SUSANNAH FIELD	aged 8 years	JOHN TENNANT	aged 11 years
JAMES FULCHER	aged 14 years	WILLIAM TENNANT	aged 10 years
ELIZABETH FULCHER	aged 15 years	HAPPY THORPE	aged 11 years
JOHN HORACE FOX	aged 19 years	WILLIAM TOWNSHEND TRORY	aged 12 years
SARAH GILBERT	aged 12 years	MARY ANN THOMPSON	aged 15 years
ALICE GOTTS	aged 52 years	LOUISE UTTING	aged 7 years
ALICE GOTTS (Jnr)	aged 9 years	SARAH UTTING	aged 18 years
WILLIAM GRIMMER	aged 8 years	CAROLINE UTTING	aged 5 years
WILLIAM HENDLE	aged 10 years	MARIA VINCENT	aged 19 years
SARAH HUNN	aged 13 years	RICHARD VINCENT	missing
ELIZABETH HUNNIBAL	aged 13 years	WILLIAM WALTER WATTS	aged 9 years
ELIZABETH HATCH	aged 12 years	EMILY YOUNG	aged 6 years
ELIZABETH JOHNSON	aged 7 years	MARTHA YALLOP	aged 20 years

Sleep thy Children, peace find thee, your stories told, your spirits free.
God bless them all. x

book and listing the names of the victims, the memorial cost £5,000 and was unveiled in September 2013. It stands by the riverside a short distance from the North West Tower.

Other stories from Great Yarmouth relating to witchcraft, murders and bodysnatching, are included in chapters 'Tales of Norfolk Witchcraft' and 'Mysterious Murders and Other Crimes'.

THE LEGEND OF KING JOHN'S LOST TREASURE

According to this ancient tale, King John's treasure was lost in the murky waters of the Wash in 1216. He and his entourage had travelled from Lincolnshire to Bishop's Lynn (now King's Lynn) in West Norfolk. He left the town with a formidable army on 11 October 1216, either heading back north or going west to Wisbech. One version of events tells us that the King overindulged in a large meal of lampreys at Wisbech Castle and was taken ill. His army and baggage train then headed north without the monarch and attempted to cross the Wash. They were said to be carrying a vast amount of money and possibly the crown jewels as well. The tide flooded in and submerged the army, entourage and valuables. Another account suggests that the King was with his men but managed to escape a watery fate. Much of the story comes from the thirteenth-century chroniclers Roger of Wendover and Matthew Paris. Though they differed on some points, they agreed that King John lost his men, packhorses, carts and priceless treasure.

King John (John Cassell, 1865).

The landscape has changed greatly over the centuries and the exact location of the catastrophe is disputed. It may have taken place in the area around Walpole Island and what is now Sutton Bridge, or possibly closer to Wisbech and Walsoken. The worst-case scenario is that up to 3,000 troops and servants plus animals were drowned, though some historians believe that if it happened at all it was probably on a much smaller scale. The 'lost treasure' element may have been woven into the tale to make it more intriguing, though it could disguise a darker truth. Also known to history as John Lackland and King John the Bad, he was by no means one of England's most popular rulers and is also associated with the legend of Robin Hood. After being forced to sign the Magna Carta at Runnymede on 19 June 1215, the King remained at odds with various powerful barons. After his death from dysentery aged forty-nine at Newark Castle in Lincolnshire on the night of 18/19 October 1216, members of his own household plundered much of his property. Whether this included the crown jewels is pure conjecture. One theory is that the treasure may have been taken and divided up to pay off the King's enormous debts. Over 800 years later it seems highly unlikely that the full truth will ever be known, but treasure hunters are still drawn to the Wash in the hope of finding a legendary fortune.

Could King John's treasure still be awaiting discovery in the Wash? (Photo: Rosalind Middleton)

THE LOST VILLAGE OF ECCLES-JUXTA-MARE

The North Sea has claimed a number of coastal settlements over the centuries and several places in Norfolk have either disappeared completely beneath the waves or been seriously diminished. With the possible exception of Shipden the lost village of Eccles is probably the best known.

Eccles-Juxta-Mare was already well established by the reign of Edward the Confessor and was recorded in the Domesday Survey of 1086. Eccles grew into one of the largest fishing villages in the area and St Mary's Church was probably built in the twelfth century. During the late sixteenth and early seventeenth centuries, a large part of the village including the church was destroyed by the sea. By 1604 at the latest only the steeple remained intact, though substantial ruins of the remainder of the church may have been visible for many years. During the early nineteenth century the steeple was engulfed by sand with just the top half still visible. The full tower almost miraculously reappeared on Christmas Day in 1862, following severe gales which also uncovered other parts of the church plus ruined houses, roads and ditches. Scouring tides continued to expose walls and foundations during the 1870s and '80s. For the first time in centuries the churchyard was laid bare and coffins could be seen.

Now on the beach and at the mercy of the sea and winds, the steeple finally succumbed to the elements and fell on the evening of 22 January 1895.

Eccles Church tower, late nineteenth century. (Illustration by Emily Middleton, courtesy of John Middleton)

Church ruins (top) and a skeleton (bottom) on Eccles beach in 1991.

The sands soon began to cover its remains but further scouring tides in the years that followed revealed much of the churchyard and other areas of the site. Up to thirty-six skeletons could be seen after such tides between 1912 and 1914, which resulted in widespread looting of skulls and bones. Medical students were blamed along with sightseers who took home macabre mementos of their visit.

The church ruins were mainly covered with sand between the early 1920s and mid-1980s. Parts of the site were uncovered in early 1986, and in April 1991 huge waves removed much of the sand to reveal previously hidden areas of the churchyard and mediaeval village. This scour again revealed skeletons on the beach and as before it attracted many visitors and led to the removal of bones. The previously unpublished photographs give an idea of how much was visible during this period. Massive granite reefs were built offshore during the 1990s to help protect against further erosion, and since then the secrets of Eccles beach have largely been covered by sand. The churchyard is still consecrated ground and for many years a beach service has been held annually on the last Sunday in August. Fishermen once claimed that church bells could be heard ringing beneath the sea at Eccles, but it seems that they fell silent long ago.

SHIPDEN AND OTHER LOST VILLAGES

The ancient village of Shipden lies beneath the waves just beyond the present Cromer Pier. At the time of the Domesday Survey in 1086 the village had a population of 117. Buildings included a manor house and two churches, one of which served the nearby settlements of Shipden-juxta-Felbrigg and Crowmere. St Peter's, the main village church, was lost to the sea around the mid-fourteenth century after the churchyard had already disappeared, and the remainder of Shipden was later doomed to a watery grave.

As at Eccles, it was long claimed that church bells could be heard ringing beneath the waves at Shipden and that this was a warning of bad weather. The top of the tower, known as Church Rock, could still be seen at low tide during the eighteenth century. It made its presence known in August 1888, when a pleasure steamer named the *Victoria* struck it and became impaled. The vessel regularly made the round trip from Great Yarmouth to Cromer and back carrying up to 100 paying passengers, but this would be its last voyage. All passengers and crew were rescued but it proved impossible to dislodge the *Victoria*. Eventually it was decided to resort to dynamite and the steamer was blown to smithereens along with the top section of Church Rock. In recent times the wreckage plus evidence of old Shipden has been found by divers. It is claimed that mysterious mirages of the submerged village occasionally appear above the waves.

Other underwater Norfolk villages include Clare, Foulness, Keswick, Waxham Parva and Newton. Land erosion is still a major problem on the Norfolk coast today with wind and waves taking their inevitable toll. Much land has been lost at Happisburgh where the famous lighthouse is now much closer to the cliff edge than it once was. Along the coast at Hemsby near Great Yarmouth, several homes

The submerged village of Shipden is located just beyond Cromer Pier.

were destroyed in 2018. Some toppled over the edge onto the beach below and others were demolished before they could follow suit.

SMUGGLING AND PIRACY

Smuggling or 'free trading' was rife on the east coast during the seventeenth and eighteenth centuries. Highly taxed commodities such as alcohol, tobacco, tea and lace, were the smugglers' stock in trade and provided them with a lucrative living. It was, of course, a very dangerous occupation and clashes between the lawbreakers and the authorities were commonplace. Large-scale smuggling by ruthless organised gangs brought a swift response and soldiers were often deployed. Twenty-six-year-old William Webb from the 15th Dragoons was killed on 26 September 1784. His gravestone in the churchyard at Old Hunstanton tells us that he 'was shot from his horse by a party of smugglers'. *The Norfolk Chronicle* dated 8 February 1783 reported an incident at Thornham where an estimated 200 smugglers unloaded their cargo in full view of a few revenue officers who had no military back-up and were powerless to intervene. The authorities had more success during a skirmish at sea in 1817, when revenue men onboard *Ranger* stopped a smugglers' ship loaded with contraband tobacco, spirits and other items.

There is no doubt that smugglers on the wild North Sea coast used the Black Shuck legend (*see* 'Strange and Spooky Tales') to their advantage to keep locals at bay when conducting nefarious business at night. They disguised various animals to look like huge demon dogs – at least from a distance. The area

Happisburgh was one of many smuggling hotspots on the Norfolk coast.

between Weybourne and Sheringham was popular with smugglers as a good spot to land contraband. Several windmillers along the Norfolk coast, including one at Weybourne, would stop their mills' sails in a particular position to warn 'free traders' of the presence of revenue men. Another smuggling hotspot was between Eccles-on-Sea and Happisburgh, with the illicit cargo being brought ashore at Cart Gap. Writing about Eccles, the late historian and author W. H. Cooke states, 'The Sand Hills here have secreted much valuable property with little fear of detection, being safer than holes made in cliffs.'

At Happisburgh (pronounced 'Hazebro') the rotting corpse of a man was found at the bottom of a well during the eighteenth century. The body had been cut into several pieces and the head was attached only by a thin strip of flesh at the back. A dispute between smugglers had escalated into violence with tragic consequences. According to a local legend the well was searched after a horrible apparition of the murdered man appeared nearby. Another gruesome tale relates to a coastguardsman who once patrolled the old coast path linking Mundesley and Bacton. On one dark night during the early 1800s, he bravely confronted a smuggling gang in the mistaken belief that back-up in the form of troops was about to arrive. As he shone his lamp the gang attacked and savagely killed him. His body was cut up and thrown into the sea, leaving no trace. Inevitably, it is claimed that his restless spirit still haunts the area.

In addition to smuggling, the sea off the Norfolk coast was once plagued by pirates. King James I granted a charter to Great Yarmouth in 1608, permitting the trial of alleged pirates. The first such trial in the town took place on 25 March 1613, which resulted in three men being found guilty of piracy and subsequently hanged. Edward Charter, Thomas Jinkins and Michael Muggs were convicted of capturing the *Seahorse* and her cargo of herrings, lamprey and beer. They were arrested after sailing into Great Yarmouth harbour. A number of other piracy trials followed in the town during the seventeenth century and the last took place as late as 1823. The body of notorious pirate William Paine, who was put to death in London in 1781, was chained to a gibbet on the North Denes in Great Yarmouth for more than twenty years as a deterrent to others.

SHIPWRECKS AND RESCUES

Shipwrecks and rescues on the Norfolk coast over the centuries are numerous, and some of the stories are certainly worthy of inclusion here.

St Mary's churchyard, Happisburgh, holds the remains of many shipwrecked sailors. Thirty-two members of the crew of HMS *Peggy* were buried here after the ship ran aground on 19 December 1770. The ironically named HMS *Invincible*, launched in March 1765, was wrecked off Happisburgh on 16 March 1801 and sank the following day. It was on its way from Great Yarmouth to join Admiral Nelson's fleet at Copenhagen but was blown off course. Around 400 men were killed and 119 were interred in a mass grave beneath a green mound on the

Memorials to the crews of HMS *Invincible* (left) and *Young England* (right), Happisburgh churchyard.

HENRY BLOGG
G.C. B.E.M.
COXSWAIN OF CROMER
LIFE-BOATS 1909-1947
WINNER OF THE R.N.L.I.
GOLD MEDAL
FOR CONSPICUOUS
GALLANTRY 3 TIMES
OF ITS SILVER MEDAL
4 TIMES
WITH THE HELP OF
HIS GALLANT CREW
RESCUED 873 LIVES
DURING 53 YEARS
OF SERVICE
'ONE OF THE
BRAVEST MEN
WHO EVER LIVED'
DIED JUNE 13TH 1954

Henry Blogg's memorial, Cromer.

north side of the churchyard. A memorial stone was placed there in 1998. Three years after the HMS *Invincible* tragedy, a revenue cutter named HMS *Hunter* floundered in the same area. Most of her crew died and were also buried at Happisburgh. A barque called *Young England* was wrecked off Winterton-on-Sea in 1876 and six members of her crew joined the ranks of sailors who sleep in the churchyard. A headstone in the form of an anchor marks their grave. The wreck of the *Ever Hopeful* at Salthouse in January 1709 is inextricably linked with the legend of Black Shuck.

Henry Blogg GC BEM (6 February 1876–13 June 1954), legendary coxswain of the Cromer lifeboat, helped rescue 873 souls in 387 launches. He first became coxswain in 1909 and retired in 1947, aged seventy-one. A crab fisherman, Blogg served the RNLI for a total of fifty-three years and was awarded the British Empire Medal and the George Cross in recognition of his bravery. He and his crew rescued thirty men and a dog after the steamer *Nevoso* was wrecked on the notorious Haisborough Sands in 1932. Nine years later, during the Second World War, he and his men picked up forty-four survivors from the *English Trader*, which ran aground in a similar position. The RNLI Henry Blogg Museum opened on Cromer seafront in 2006 and contains a lifeboat used by him plus many other exhibits. A memorial to Henry Blogg stands in North Lodge Park and the inscription describes him as 'one of the bravest men who ever lived'.

MERMAIDS AND OTHER FISHY TALES

The mermaid legend is one of Norfolk's oldest and strangest. For centuries the mermaid was considered a reality in many cultures and became part of Norfolk's coastal folklore. Usually said to take the form of a woman from the waist up but with the scaly tail of a fish, mermaids were mentioned by Pliny the Elder in his *Historia Naturalis* in the first century AD. Christopher Columbus is said to have seen three of the creatures near Haiti in 1493, and Captain John Smith (allegedly 'saved' by Pocahontas) reported seeing one with green hair in 1614! In fiction, William Shakespeare referred to 'a mermaid on a dolphin's back' in *A Midsummer Night's Dream* and Hans Christian Anderson wrote *The Little Mermaid* in 1836. Early illustrations and carvings bear little resemblance to the modern image of the glamorous mermaid as portrayed by Daryl Hannah in the film *Splash* (1984).

Reports of mermaids in Norfolk date back to the twelfth century and wooden carvings depicting them can be seen in several of the county's churches including Upper Sheringham, Cley and Grimston. The carving inside All Saints Church, Upper Sheringham, is situated on a fifteenth-century pew and is supposed to record a real event of an exhausted mermaid who was refused entry to the church by a beadle during a service. She later managed to gain access when nobody was looking and rested on the pew closest to the north door, where her image can still be seen. Communities close to Norfolk's north and north-west coast have the greatest tradition of mermaid activity with the area around the Wash said to be the most likely place to see one. Mermaid Sand near the village of Snettisham is named after a dark-haired siren seen there long ago.

A mermaid carving in Cley Church.

According to legend the mermaid or sea-woman could magically discard her tail and transform herself into a normal female with the usual number of lower limbs. This enabled her to leave the sea and interact with the local community and even marry unsuspecting mortals. Though always naked in her natural habitat she would modestly wear clothes while on land. The lure of life beneath the waves often became too much for the mermaid to resist and several returned to their former lives. Some are said to have led besotted men to a watery grave with their enchanting song. Mermen have also been reported, perhaps the most famous such case being that of the Wild Man of Orford who was caught off the Suffolk coast around 1167 and imprisoned in the castle. He eventually escaped and returned to the sea, though most accounts indicate that he had legs instead of a tail.

Possible explanations for mermaid sightings include manatees or dugongs, seals (very prevalent on the Norfolk coast), mirages caused by unusual weather conditions, real women bathing, partly submerged boulders, intoxication, deliberate hoaxes and over-active imaginations. Several unsubstantiated claims have been made of mermaids being captured alive from the sea or being washed up dead and intermittent reports continue to the present day. A group of fishermen reported capturing one alive off the Norfolk coast in 1832 and a similar incident involved a father and son fishing near Winterton. In both cases the unusual catch was given back to the deep. In recent times there have been a number of reports from around the world of unexplained creatures being washed up following extreme weather events. Several national and local newspapers carried a story in October 2016 that the body of an alleged mermaid had been found on Great Yarmouth beach. A witness, who uploaded intriguing photos and a shaky video to social media, was described in one report as 'a keen creator of models' who specialised in 'fish-themed pieces of art!'

A resting mermaid in Upper Sheringham Church.

Extraordinary True-life Stories

Many historical characters with Norfolk connections, both well known and more obscure, have interesting stories to tell. Several were born and bred in the county while others were 'outsiders' who made their homes here. Some, such as the internationally famous Pocahontas or the little-known Father Ignatius, were temporary visitors who nevertheless left their mark on local folklore. The following is a personal selection which avoids some of the more obvious names whose stories have been told many times.

TALL TALES: THE NORFOLK GIANT

The fascinating story of the man best known as the Norfolk Giant has many twists and turns and there are times when the line between fact and fiction becomes blurred. Robert Hales was born in West Somerton on 2 May 1813, and over the next fifty years his stature and fame grew to such an extent that he was well known on both sides of the Atlantic and mixed with royalty. Billed as the 'Tallest Man in Europe', according to contemporary accounts he stood 7 feet 8 inches (2.35 metres) high and weighed up to 33 stone (210 kg). Robert was one of nine children born to William and Elizabeth Hales and the whole family were tall. His father and mother were 6 feet 6 inches (2 metres) and 6 feet (1.8 metres) tall respectively, and his eight siblings were all over 6 feet tall.

Robert Hales enlisted in the Royal Navy aged just thirteen but his promising career was cut short four years later as his rapidly increasing height made it difficult for him to fit below the decks of vessels. Suddenly finding himself without employment, he made appearances at local fairs including Tombland in Norwich and at Great Yarmouth's Britannia Pier. He then went on to tour Britain and was introduced to Queen Victoria and Prince Albert at Epsom in 1840. He also met the Duke of Wellington and Louis Philippe of France. Hales toured far and wide, sometimes with his sisters Mary and Anne, who were around 7 feet 2 inches (2.2 metres) and 6 feet 9 inches (2.05 metres) tall respectively, but they both died young during the 1840s.

Between 1849 and 1851, Robert Hales undertook a lucrative tour of the United States and worked for the legendary P. T. Barnham, who is said to have paid him £800. During this period he 'married' an Irish giantess named Elizabeth Simpson in a much-publicised and very elaborate ceremony. This was probably a huge publicity stunt by Barnham and Hales later returned home a rich man,

ROBERT HALES, THE "NORFOLK GIANT."

Above left: Robert Hales, the Norfolk Giant. (Courtesy of the Wellcome Collection CC-BY-4.0)

Above right: Poster of the Norfolk Giant. (Courtesy of the Wellcome Collection CC-BY-4.0)

though without his 'wife'. It was rumoured that he and Simpson had a son together, though evidence is lacking. What is certain is that Hales then married Maria Webb and they were together for the remainder of his life. In 1851 the Norfolk Giant was summoned to Buckingham Palace to once again meet Queen Victoria and her husband plus their children. She presented him with a gold watch and chain. He also appeared at the Great Exhibition in London the same year.

Contemporary accounts describe Robert Hales as an intelligent, handsome and brave man. He was credited with saving a boy from drowning on his journey to America in late 1848, when he dived into the sea and hauled the youngster to safety. There is also a story that he single-handedly threw a group of men off a

The imposing grave of Robert Hales, West Somerton churchyard.

piece of land that he owned in Yorkshire. In his later years, Hales retired from touring and ran public houses in Drury Lane, London, and in Sheffield. He died from bronchitis at the age of fifty in Great Yarmouth on 22 November 1863, and was buried in St Mary's churchyard, West Somerton. His elaborate sarcophagus was restored in the early twenty-first century. Beside it are the graves of other members of his remarkably tall family in this tranquil 'churchyard of the giants'.

HOWARD CARTER, TUTANKHAMUN – AND NORFOLK

It is common knowledge that the tomb of the Egyptian Pharaoh Tutankhamun was finally discovered and opened by British archaeologist Howard Carter after lying undisturbed for over 3,000 years. Carter's strong Norfolk links are less well understood, particularly outside his home county. Although born in Kensington, London, on 9 May 1874, he was brought up in Swaffham where his parents, Samuel and Martha, were born. Carter's infatuation with ancient Egypt was triggered by artefacts he encountered as a child at Didlington Hall. His father, a talented artist, was commissioned by Lord and Lady Amherst to paint portraits of their animals and the young Howard went along too. Lord Amherst was a keen collector and was happy to pass on his knowledge to the boy.

After securing a post at the British Museum, Carter began working in Egypt while still a teenager. His famous association with Lord Carnarvon began in 1907 during tomb excavations near Thebes (now Luxor), but it would be another fifteen years before the Norfolk man made the greatest archaeological discovery of the twentieth century. The First World War interrupted excavations in the Valley of the Kings, but Carter returned in late 1917 and continued searching for an elusive tomb that he believed was waiting to be discovered. In November 1922, Carter and his party finally found the 'missing' tomb, though the burial chamber was not entered until 16 February 1923.

The rest, of course, is history. Howard Carter suddenly became internationally famous and embarked on lecture tours of Britain, Europe and the United States. He died from Hodgkin's disease at the age of sixty-four on 2 March 1939, and was buried in Putney Vale Cemetery, London. Some believe that Lord Carnarvon and perhaps even Carter himself succumbed to the fabled 'curse' of Tutankhamen. Nearly a century on from his greatest find, Carter is well remembered in Swaffham as a local lad who went on to make history. The town's museum has a room dedicated to his life and work, along with many Egyptian artefacts.

The Howard Carter Room, Swaffham Museum. (Courtesy of Swaffham Heritage)

FROM PULPIT TO LION'S DEN

The peculiar, sometimes outrageous, and ultimately tragic story of a former Norfolk rector proves that fact really can be stranger than fiction. Harold Davidson was born in Sholing, Hampshire, on 14 July 1875, the son of the local vicar. After following his father into the Anglican Church, he was appointed rector of Stiffkey-cum-Morston in North Norfolk in 1906, a position he held for twenty-six years. As time went by, Davidson spent an increasing amount of time in London fulfilling his unofficial duties as the self-styled 'Prostitute's Padre'. He would spend up to six days a week in the capital and befriended many young women he found working on the streets, in theatres, and in teashops. A number of these were invited back to the twenty-roomed Stiffkey rectory, which did not always go down well with Davidson's wife Molly or some of his parishioners! His great desire to save 'fallen' women was apparently sparked by an incident in 1894 when he claimed to have rescued a sixteen-year-old girl from drowning herself in the River Thames.

After one of Harold Davidson's parishioners, Major Hamond, made an official complaint to the Bishop of Norwich concerning the vicar's alleged misconduct, he was tried by a consistory court. The trial took several weeks and heard evidence from many of the young women befriended by Davidson. A photograph was

Stiffkey Church, where Harold Davidson was Rector between 1906 and 1932.

produced which showed the vicar with a semi-naked teenage girl, an incident that was probably staged by the press to help sell newspapers. Davidson was found guilty of immorality and Bishop Pollock decided that he should be defrocked. An appeal failed but for three months after the verdict Davidson continued to take services at Stiffkey Church and proclaim his innocence. The juicy story was covered by many national newspapers and magazines. Numerous reporters arrived in the village and Davidson willingly gave many interviews.

Harold Davidson delivered his last church sermon on 21 August 1932, to a packed congregation. The former rector's next move was typically eccentric as he reinvented himself as a side-show act. He entertained holidaymakers from inside a small barrel in Blackpool and performed other demeaning stunts over a five-year period. Davidson's last employment was at Captain Rye's Pavilion in Skegness, Lincolnshire, where he was booked for the 1937 summer season. After delivering a ten-minute sermon in which he strongly criticised the Church for 'unjustly' treating him, he would spend two to three minutes locked in a cage with lions. Everything had gone as planned until the evening of 28 July 1937, when it all went horribly wrong. After stepping into the cage he cracked his whip at a male lion, which reared up, knocked Davidson to the ground and stalked around the cage

Harold Davidson's grave, Stiffkey churchyard.

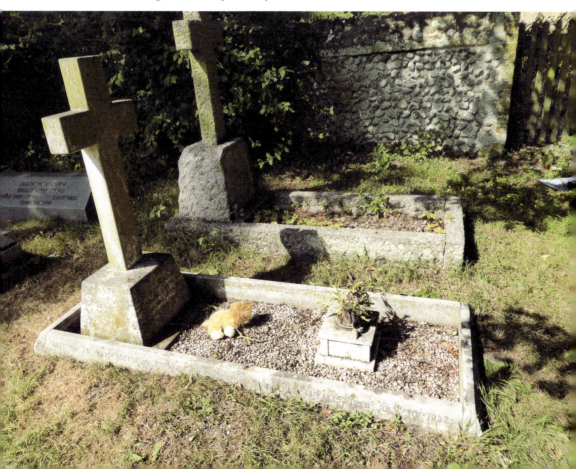

with him in its jaws. A slightly different version has it that he accidently stepped on the creature's tail. The lion tamer, a short-sighted sixteen-year-old girl (!) named Irene Somner, rushed in and bravely pulled the former vicar from the cage. He died from his injuries two days later, aged sixty-two.

Harold Davidson was buried in the churchyard at Stiffkey and his funeral attracted many mourners and sightseers. When I visited in 2018, a stuffed toy lion had been placed on his grave. I suspect he would have appreciated the irony! In recent years there have been calls for Davidson to be posthumously cleared of any wrongdoing.

POCAHONTAS: THE NORFOLK CONNECTION

Most people are probably familiar with the traditional tale of Pocahontas as popularised by Disney, but many fewer will be aware that Norfolk played a part in her tragically short real-life story. The daughter of Chief Powhatan, she was born in Virginia around 1595/6 and was named Matoaka but also known as Amonute. The name by which she is now universally famous was a nickname meaning 'the mischievous one'.

According to legend, in December 1607 an eleven- or twelve-year-old Pocahontas fearlessly saved the life of Captain John Smith, who was about to be killed by her father. The incident is remembered in the lyrics of the song *Fever*, popularised by Peggy Lee. Some historians believe the story was either an exaggeration of real events or a complete fabrication invented by Smith. In 1613 Pocahontas was taken prisoner by the British and converted to Christianity. She was baptized and changed her name to Rebecca.

In April 1614 she married Norfolk man John Rolfe and moved to England with him and their twelve-month-old child Thomas two years later. They spent at least part of their short marriage at Heacham Hall in the west of the county, where Pocahontas is said to have planted a mulberry tree which still survives. A memorial to her can be seen in St Mary's Church and she is also remembered on Heacham village sign. While living in England she was introduced to King James I and also visited the Globe Theatre to watch some of William Shakespeare's plays. Her status as a Native American princess made her a sensation at social gatherings.

Sadly, Rebecca Rolfe became seriously ill and died in Gravesend, Kent, in March 1617, aged just twenty-one or twenty-two. She and her husband were about to leave England for a trip back to Virginia and according to some accounts had already boarded a ship. Rebecca – or Pocahontas as she will eternally be known – was buried on 21 March 1617 in the chancel of St George's Church, Gravesend, and her statue now stands in the churchyard. Her death has variously been attributed to consumption, pneumonia, smallpox, or even poisoning. After his wife's death, John Rolfe returned to Virginia as planned but was killed in 1622 aged around thirty-seven. He never again saw his son Thomas, who was brought up at Heacham Hall by his uncle, Henry Rolfe. Thomas also later returned to America, where he died around 1680.

Heacham village sign features
one-time resident Pocahontas.
(Uksignpix CC-BY-SA-3.0)

PABLO FANQUE AND THE BEATLES

The true-life story of the man born William Darby in Norwich reads like a work
of fiction with elements of hardship, mystery, theatre, fame and tragedy. He
was one of the top circus performers of his time and the first black owner of
a British circus. Nearly a century after his death he received recognition, under
his pseudonym Pablo Fanque, on one of the most influential pop/rock albums
of all time.

Originally billed as 'Young Darby', his public debut with William Batty's Circus
was in his home city on 26 December 1821, when he may have been just eleven
years old. He later became an accomplished horse rider, trainer, rope walker and
tumbler. By 1834 Darby was using the stage name Pablo Fanque and started his
eponymous travelling circus around 1840.

Pablo Fanque's blue plaque, Norwich.

A tragic accident took the life of Darby's first wife Susannah, who was killed when a temporary 600-seater gallery collapsed during a circus performance in Leeds on 18 March 1848. Mrs Darby, who was forty-seven years old, was the only fatality but a number of people were injured. William Darby is said to have remarried just three months later, his second wife being a circus horse rider named Elizabeth Corker who was in her early twenties. When William died from bronchitis in Stockport on 4 May 1871, he was buried in Leeds with his first wife.

According to his gravestone Darby was seventy-five years old, though some argue that his true age was actually sixty-one. It is known that a William Darby was born in Norwich to John and Mary Darby in 1796 – which ties in with his claimed age – but this child died the following year. Another William Darby was born on 30 March 1810 at the city's St Andrew's Workhouse to parents with identical names. Census records appear to support the theory that the child who grew up to be Pablo Fanque was the second William Darby – probably the younger brother of the baby who died – though historians and authors are still split on this issue.

Pablo Fanque was immortalised in the Beatles song *Being for the Benefit of Mr Kite*, featured on the group's iconic 1967 record *Sgt Pepper's Lonely Hearts*

The 1843 poster that inspired a song by the Beatles.

Club Band. The composition was inspired by a poster purchased by John Lennon from an antiques shop in Kent. It advertised a benefit show by Pablo Fanque's Circus Royal for performer William Kite at Town Meadows, Rochdale, in 1843. A blue plaque was placed on the John Lewis department store in Norwich in 2010, close to Darby's early home in Ber Street. The Beatles – who played at the Grosvenor Rooms in Prince of Wales Road, Norwich, on 17 May 1963 – have their own blue plaque which records that they queued for chips with fans after the gig, less than a year before they conquered America and achieved worldwide success.

A MEDIEVAL MYSTIC AND AUTHOR

Few facts are known relating to the medieval anchoress, author and mystic known variously as Mother, Lady or Dame Julian. Some sources state that she was a member of the Benedictine order in Norwich, but others believe she was a laywoman. Often referred to simply as Julian of Norwich, her life up to the age of thirty remains shrouded in mystery. She is thought to have been born in or around the city in late 1342 but almost died in 1373 and was given the last rites. It was at this time that she experienced a total of sixteen visions of Jesus Christ before being declared cured of her illness on 13 May.

From around 1374/5 she voluntarily spent the rest of her life in a small room or cell at St Julian's Church (located between King Street and Rouen Road in Norwich) as an anchoress – a woman who lives in solitude and dedicates her life

Above left: Julian's cell, St Julian's Church, Norwich.

Above right: Statue of Julian of Norwich by David Holgate, Norwich Cathedral West Front. (Courtesy of Norwich Cathedral)

to God. Julian's real name is unknown but she appears to have simply taken the name of the church where she sought refuge. Her visions were the inspiration for *Revelations of Devine Love,* considered to be the earliest English language book written by a woman. Some of the beliefs expressed were at odds with contemporary Catholicism but it is now regarded as an important theological work. In essence, Julian believed that God loved everybody regardless of their failings and that 'all shall be well and all manner of thing shall be well'.

Julian's cell is thought to have had a window looking into the church to allow her to witness services. She probably conversed with others through another window looking out on the churchyard. The original cell was demolished after the Reformation and the church suffered severe bomb damage during the Second World War. A replica of Julian's cell was constructed in 1952 as part of the rebuilt church and serves as a chapel and shrine dedicated to her memory. Modern pilgrims and visitors should be grateful that the replica has a feature that the original lacked: a large doorway to enable easy entry and exit. An inscription inside the cell states, 'Here dwelt Mother Julian, Anchoress of Norwich, c.1342-1430'. Some historians believe that Julian probably died around 1416, though whichever date is correct, by the standards of the time hers was a very long life.

A FAMOUS 'BENTLEY BOY'

Visitors to Blakeney churchyard on the North Norfolk coast may wonder what story lies behind a modest grave bearing the words 'A racing motorist of international fame'. It is perhaps an unlikely resting place for a man who in his day was almost as well known as the modern heroes of Formula One.

Sir Henry Ralph Stanley Birkin, 3rd Baronet, also known as 'Tim', was a gentleman racer and one of the famous 'Bentley Boys'. He was born in Nottingham in 1896 but developed a love of Norfolk and purchased the Tacolneston Hall estate. He spent his honeymoon at Blakeney and was president of the Blakeney Royal Lifeboat Institution. Birkin enjoyed a successful career as a racing driver in the late 1920s and early 1930s. He won the Brooklands six-hour race in 1928 and finished first at Le Mans in 1929 with co-driver Woolf Barnato.

Sir Henry crossed swords with Walter Owen Bentley, the firm's founder, when with outside assistance he helped develop a supercharged car called the Bentley Blower No. 1. Although the car proved to be unreliable, as W. O. had predicted, Birkin finally talked him into producing fifty supercharged cars to enable the model to be entered in the Le Mans twenty-four-hour race of 1930. Two works 'blower' Bentleys started the race but neither finished. Later the same year he finished as runner-up in the French Grand Prix. The company made huge losses in the wake of the Wall Street crash of 1929 and was taken over by Rolls-Royce in 1931. Birkin won at Le Mans that year, but in an Alfa Romeo rather than a Bentley. He rebuilt Blower No. 1 as a single-seater racer after the original two-seater fabric body caught fire in 1929, and set a new Brooklands outer circuit track record of 137.96 mph (222.02 km/h) in 1932. Birkin finished third

Sir Henry Birkin's modest grave, Blakeney churchyard.

in the Tripoli Grand Prix of 1933 driving a Maserati, but this was destined to be the gentleman racer's swansong. He died on 22 June 1933, aged thirty-six, probably from lead poisoning after burning his arm on the car's exhaust pipe while attempting to light a cigarette after the race.

Sir Henry Birkin's funeral took place on 26 June 1933, and among the many mourners was the legendary land and water speed record-breaker Sir Malcolm Campbell. Actor Rowan Atkinson played the part of Sir Henry in a television drama titled *Full Throttle* in 1995, inspired by a book of the same name written by Birkin in 1932. Bentley Blower No. 1 was sold by auctioneers Bonhams at the Goodwood Festival of Speed in June 2012. It fetched £5,042,000, a record for a British-built car at a public auction.

THOMAS BROWNE'S 'MISSING' SKULL

Thousands pass by a statue of Sir Thomas Browne in Hay Hill, Norwich, every day, yet most will have little or no idea of the story behind it. Born in London in 1605, Thomas Browne relocated to Norwich in 1637 and started practising medicine in the city. He was also an influential author who wrote books and papers on many subjects including medicine, science, religion, philosophy and natural history. Many of Browne's views were at odds with contemporary thinking and somewhat eccentric by modern standards. He was an avid collector of birds' eggs and his house was full of curiosities including a stuffed dolphin and

Statue of Sir Thomas Browne
with feathered friends, Hay Hill,
Norwich.

a live Bittern. Browne believed in witchcraft and spoke at the trial of two women accused of the practice in Bury St Edmunds, Suffolk, around 1662. They were found guilty and put to death.

Thomas Browne was knighted when King Charles II visited Norwich in 1671. He died on 19 October 1682 and was buried in the chancel of the imposing St Peter Mancroft Church, where his memorial can be seen to the right of the High Altar. Despite strongly criticising the theft of bones and skulls from graves, Browne's own sleep was disturbed in 1840 when his lead coffin was accidentally damaged by workmen. His skull was controversially removed and presented to the museum of the Norfolk and Norwich Hospital. Ironically, it had still not been returned to St Peter Mancroft when a statue by Henry Alfred Pegram was erected close to the church in 1905 to commemorate the bicentenary of Browne's birth. The statue is a popular perch for local pigeons and depicts the great 'thinker' in pensive pose with a broken burial urn in his outstretched right hand. After photographs and casts were taken, Browne's skull was finally reunited with his other mortal remains in 1922.

FATHER IGNATIUS AND HIS PRIORY

A blue plaque on the wall of a house in Norwich's historic Elm Hill commemorates Father Ignatius, a shadowy and controversial figure in the street's history. Born in London in 1837, his real name was Joseph Lyne and he had already clashed with church authorities in various parts of the country before arriving in Norwich. Lyne put down a deposit on No. 14 Elm Hill, which at that time was in a dilapidated state, and opened the Benedictine Priory of St Mary and St Dunstan around 1863/4. Now calling himself Father Ignatius, he soon became a very divisive figure, attracting both fanatical support and strong opposition. To his supporters he was a great healer who had the ability to cure the sick, but his critics condemned him as a dangerous maverick. Father Ignatius dressed in a monk's habit and carried a large black bible. He became notorious for publically cursing those he regarded as sinners. It was claimed that at least three people he cursed died suddenly, including a woman who apparently expired on the spot outside the priory!

Following various accusations against Ignatius and his associates and a bitter dispute regarding ownership of the building, the priory closed in 1866. He was ordered to leave the property but later managed to regain access on two occasions before finally being evicted. One account states that he was physically removed from his bed and the city itself by an angry mob and warned never to return. It is recorded, however, that he made further visits to Norwich during the 1890s and preached to large congregations of loyal followers.

After opening another short-lived priory in London, Father Ignatius moved to Wales where he founded Llanthony Abbey in 1869. Here he lived until his death in 1908. Despite being laid to rest in the grounds of his abbey, the ghost of Father Ignatius has been reported in Elm Hill, still carrying his bible and angrily cursing passing 'sinners'.

Entrance to the former priory, Elm Hill, Norwich.

Tales of Norfolk Witchcraft

The belief in witchcraft was widespread for hundreds of years and Norfolk was far from unique in persecuting and executing alleged practitioners. It was often older women, particularly those who lived alone and kept black cats or other small creatures as pets, who were accused of witchcraft. Nevertheless, a number of younger women and some men were also convicted and executed. The traditional method of trying a person believed to be a witch was by the so-called 'swimming'. This often involved tying a rope around the accused's neck and binding their hands and feet before lowering them into a river or lake. If they floated, they were judged to be guilty of witchcraft and sentenced to death.

Witch 'swimming' took place at Fye Bridge, Norwich.

If they drowned, they were pronounced innocent. Amazingly, this catch-22 situation was considered a fair and just way of determining a person's guilt. A formal trial of sorts was sometimes held but the odds were stacked against the accused and flimsy or concocted evidence was often sufficient to ensure the death sentence. In Norfolk, most convicted witches were hanged but some were burned to death.

In Norwich, a ducking chair was installed at Fye Bridge over the River Wensum to enable the 'swimming' of suspected witches. Lollard's Pit, on what is now Riverside Road in Norwich, was an infamous place of execution by burning, where violent death was served up as public entertainment for large crowds. The word 'Lollard' may have come from the Dutch for 'mumbler'. It is thought that at least fifty people were killed at Lollard's Pit, some burned as witches and others as dissenters or heretics. Executions at the former chalk pit, where material was excavated to form the foundations of Norwich Cathedral, started in the early fifteenth century and continued until the late sixteenth century. Four young women convicted of witchcraft were executed there in the late sixteenth century. One is said to have broken free and crawled up the sides of the pit several times, but on each occasion the baying mob returned her to the flames where she finally

Site of Lollard's Pit, Norwich.

succumbed. Mary Oliver was probably the last alleged witch to be burned in Norwich as late as 1659 but she met her fate in the castle ditches, a location also used to hang witches. Matthew Hopkins, the infamous self-styled 'Witchfinder General' who oversaw the torture and trial of hundreds of alleged witches throughout East Anglia, visited Norfolk in 1645, a year which saw a large increase in the numbers accused and convicted. In Norwich he is said to have attended the trial of forty supposed witches.

Those sentenced to death in Norwich were locked up in the Guildhall before being paraded through the city's narrow streets. Householders along the route were encouraged to hurl rotten fruit and vegetables and even tip the contents of their chamber pots down on the prisoners' heads! Those destined to die at Lollard's Pit often spent their last night either incarcerated in holding cells beside the pit, or in the dungeon below Cow Tower on the opposite bank of the River Wensum. After their death sentence was confirmed at the Bishop's Palace, the condemned person was handed over at the city gate and led to their fate across the river over the ancient Bishop Bridge, which still exists.

A public house for many years called the Bridge House is believed to have been built above the holding cells. In 2012 it was controversially renamed Lollard's Pit in recognition of the area's grisly past. The pit's precise location is disputed but a private car park may mark the spot where so many died. A plaque on the front wall of the pub and a memorial stone on the opposite riverbank are reminders of this dreadful episode in Norwich's history. It is hardly surprising that the pub which now bears the name of the infamous pit, and the area around it, are said to be haunted. Witnesses have reported hearing moans and screams at night, and experiencing a strange sensation of intense heat. Shadowy figures and the apparition of a burning woman have also been claimed.

Twenty miles away in Great Yarmouth, Elizabeth Butcher and Joan Lingwood were hanged as witches in 1584 and buried in St Nicholas' churchyard. Nine women and two men stood trial for witchcraft at the Great Yarmouth Tolhouse (now a museum) in 1645, after Matthew Hopkins had identified them as likely practitioners. Five women were found guilty and hanged, including Elizabeth Bradwell. She was accused of making a wax image of a boy and putting a nail through its head. Her 'victim', who had suddenly become very ill, is said to have quickly recovered. Bradwell's fate was sealed after she apparently made a full confession, though how much persuasion was required is not recorded. The other unfortunates also hanged were Alice Clesswell (or Clippwell), Bridgetta Howard, Maria Blackborne (or Blackburne) and Elizabeth Dugeon. They were all buried in St Nicholas' churchyard on 29 September 1645. Others in the town may have met a similar end but records are incomplete.

Two sisters born in Great Yarmouth were unlucky enough to be caught up in the infamous Salem Witch Trials in Massachusetts, USA. Rebecca Nurse and Mary Easty were found guilty and hanged in 1692, having lived in Salem since 1640. They left their Norfolk home in 1637 with their parents, William and Joanna Towne,

Left: A plaque records the grim history of Lollard's Pit.

Below: Suspected witches were imprisoned and tried at Great Yarmouth Tolhouse.

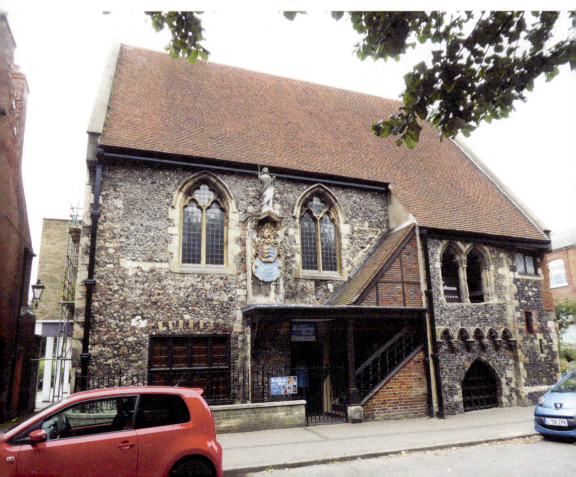

WILLIAM TOWNE and JOANNA BLESSING were married in this church on 25 April 1620 and six of their eight children were baptized here. They founded the Towne family in America. Two of their children, Rebecca and Mary, were executed during the Salem witchcraft delusion in the 1690's.

The Towne family plaque, St Nicholas Minster, Great Yarmouth.

supposedly for a better life in the New World. Another sister, Sarah Cloyce, was also arrested but not charged. Somewhat belatedly, Mary Easty's conviction was quashed twenty years after her death. A plaque recording the sisters' plight can be seen inside St Nicholas Minster where they were baptised. Members of the Towne family still living in the USA visited Great Yarmouth in 2012.

One of the seaside town's 145 narrow passageways, known collectively as the Rows, acquired an intriguing nickname by which it is still known today. Row 95, the narrowest of them all with a minimum width of just 2 feet 3 inches (0.7 metres), became known as Kittywitches or Kitty Witch Row. Alongside several rather dull theories there is a racier tale of how the unusual name may have come about. The story goes that at some unspecified date, Row 95 was home to a scary gang of women who terrorised the local area by banging on doors and threatening the inhabitants with violence if they refused to hand over money. With their faces smeared in blood and wearing men's clothing, it is unsurprising that most of their neighbours were persuaded to pay up. The women drank away their ill-gotten gains at various hostelries while their husbands were fishing at sea. They were known locally as Kitty Witches, though whether they dabbled in the black arts is uncertain. Kittywitches Row still exists between King Street and Middlegate Street but is much shorter than it once was.

In the Tuesday Market Place at King's Lynn in West Norfolk, a carving in the shape of a heart within a diamond on the front of a building serves as a reminder that this was once a place of execution. The carving is said to mark the spot where, in her death throes, the heart of a woman burst out of her body and hit the house. As usual, there are alternative versions of the tale relating to various victims and different forms of execution.

The earliest candidate as possible owner of the 'flying' heart is a maidservant named Margaret Day who was boiled alive in 1531. This horrific form of

The very narrow Kittywitches Row, Great Yarmouth.

execution, which involved repeatedly lowering the condemned person into a cauldron of water with a roaring fire beneath it, was reserved by order of Henry VIII for those found guilty of poisoning. As Margaret Day was convicted of poisoning her mistress and other family members, this would be her inevitable fate.

Nearly sixty years later, an alleged witch called Margaret Read was said to have placed a curse on a man named Nick Kirk, who died suddenly after experiencing severe chest and stomach pains. His jilted lover, who claimed to have had a child by him, was seen to visit Read shortly before he became ill. An effigy with pins in it was found in Read's house along with other incriminating evidence. Nicknamed 'Shady Meg', Read survived the ordeal of 'swimming' and was convicted of witchcraft. She was burned at the stake on 20 July 1590.

The final candidate is Mary Smith, who was executed as a witch on 12 January 1616. She cursed John Orkton, a sailor who had struck her son, and predicted that his fingers would drop off. He suddenly became ill and later had his fingers and toes amputated due to gangrene. Smith was also said to have cursed various other people including Elizabeth Hancock, who she accused of stealing one of her hens. Hancock was ill for a number of weeks before a 'cure' was found when her father consulted a local wizard or wise man. He gave instructions for the baking of a 'witch cake', containing flour and Elizabeth Hancock's urine, and also supplied special ointment and powder. Half the cake was to be applied to the patient's back and the other half to her heart. Together with other measures to remove the curse, this appears to have done the trick and Elizabeth survived. After being found guilty, Mary Smith predicted that her heart would leave her body and crash into a building used by the magistrate who had decided her fate. Different sources disagree as to whether Mary Smith was hanged or burned to death.

If the heart in question belonged to any of these three women, it is unlikely that it hit the present building that carries the mark. This was probably built in the eighteenth century, though an earlier building may have existed on the same spot. In addition to the above, a woman known as 'Mother' Gabley was hanged for witchcraft in King's Lynn during the 1580s, while Grace Wright and Dorothy Lee suffered similar fates in the 1640s.

Mysterious Murders and Other Crimes

Norfolk has had its fair share of murders and other shocking crimes. This chapter tells the stories behind four murders, plus an episode of bodysnatchings, that rocked the county.

GRUESOME MURDER ON TABERNACLE STREET

The macabre discovery of human body parts around Norwich in 1851 signalled the start of a mystery that would not be solved until almost two decades later. It began when twelve-year-old Charles Johnson was walking his dog in Lakenham Lane on 21 June 1851. The dog sniffed out what turned out to be a hand. Another hand was found by boys playing near St Peter Southgate Church. A foot was discovered by Thomas Dent's dog during a walk on Martineau Lane and another foot was found in a churchyard by Harry Layton. Sewer-men Charlie and John Sales recovered entrails, blood and flesh from a drain close to Tabernacle Street, the significance of which would only become apparent much later. Other people stumbled upon various grisly finds, all of which were passed to the police. Posters were put up around the city regarding a 'supposed murder' and requesting information about missing persons and possible suspects. It was stated that the remains were those of 'a young female between the ages of sixteen and twenty-six'. Though the sex of the victim was correct, the age range would turn out to be wildly inaccurate. The police followed up a few leads which proved inconclusive and with no head to examine, the lines of enquiry quickly dried up. The body parts were buried in a vault beneath Norwich Guildhall. One possibility considered likely at the time was that the whole episode was a hoax perpetrated by medical students with access to a dead body.

Fast forward to the evening of 1 January 1869, when William Sheward presented himself at Carter Street Police Station in Walworth, South London, and blurted out a very strange confession to Inspector William Davies. Sheward stated that he had murdered his first wife on 14/15 June 1851 and dismembered her body. He had then gone out with a bucket on several nights and disposed of her remains at various locations around Norwich. Martha Sheward, who was fifteen years older than her husband, was aged fifty-four at the time of her brutal death.

Site of the demolished Tabernacle Street, Bishopgate, Norwich.

Their marriage was punctuated by frequent angry arguments but the final one culminated in William Sheward slitting Martha's throat with a razor at their home at No. 7 Tabernacle Street (later demolished and now part of Bishopgate). In the evenings that followed he boiled his wife's head, hands and feet before inexpertly cutting up her body into small pieces and distributing it across the city.

Tailor turned pawnbroker William Sheward started drinking heavily after the murder to help block out his guilt. He married Charlotte Buck on 13 February 1862 and the couple had three children together. Before he walked into the London police station in 1869, he had been wandering around the capital with a razor in his pocket. Having failed to find the courage to end his own life, Sheward finally handed himself in. He was hanged at the old Norwich City Gaol (where the Roman Catholic cathedral now stands) on 20 April 1869. Sheward, who at the age of fifty-seven looked much older and was severely afflicted with rheumatism, had to be carried to the scaffold where Executioner Calcroft was waiting for him.

MYSTERIOUS MURDERS ON GREAT YARMOUTH BEACH

An element of mystery still surrounds two almost identical murders committed twelve years apart on the same stretch of beach at Great Yarmouth.

Fourteen-year-old John Norton saw a woman who appeared to be asleep on the South Beach at around 6.15 a.m. on Sunday 23 September 1900. He soon realised that all was not well and notified PC Manship, who was on duty some distance away. The police officer accompanied the boy to the crime scene and confirmed that the woman was deceased. A shoe lace was tied tightly around her throat.

The victim fitted the description of a woman who had been staying in lodgings at Row 104 in the town along with her young daughter. Known to her landlady Mrs Rudrum as 'Mrs Hood', the dead woman was in fact twenty-three-year-old Mary Jane Bennett from London. Suspicion fell on Herbert John Bennett, her twenty-one-year-old estranged husband. He was charged with Mary's murder and his trial began at the Old Bailey on 25 February 1901. The prosecution claimed that a gold chain found at Herbert

Left: Row 104, Great Yarmouth; *right*: Mary Jane Bennett's grave, Great Yarmouth cemetery.

Bennett's lodgings was the one worn by his wife in Great Yarmouth just before her death. It was also disclosed that he had become engaged to a parlour maid named Alice Meadows, who had no idea that he was a married man with a child. Bennett swore that he was at work at the Royal Arsenal in London around the time of his wife's murder and time sheets were produced that appeared to confirm this. However, two men who Bennett said he was drinking with in Woolwich later that evening both denied the claim. Furthermore, several witnesses came forward to testify that a man fitting Bennett's description had been seen in Great Yarmouth on 22 September 1900, including a waiter at the Crown and Anchor Hotel. William Reade stated that the accused stayed there overnight on that date. To add further confusion, a London businessman testified that he had a drink with a man he believed to be Bennett in the Bexley area on the evening of 22 September.

Herbert Bennett did not take the stand and was found guilty of murder by a jury. He was executed and buried in an unmarked grave at Norwich Prison on 21 March 1901. The prison flagpole broke when the black flag was raised to confirm that the death sentence had been carried out. Some regarded this curious incident as casting further doubt on Bennett's guilt. Even at the last he refused to confess to his wife's murder. Mary Jane Bennett lies buried in the north-west section of Great Yarmouth cemetery.

The body of another young woman, later identified as eighteen-year-old Dora May Gray, was found on Great Yarmouth beach in the early hours of Monday 15 July 1912. She too had been strangled with a shoe lace apparently from one of her own shoes. Her stockings had been removed and tied round her throat beneath the shoelace. Miss Gray's corpse was found around 400 yards from the site of the earlier murder. Her gloves were located some distance away almost opposite the monument to Lord Nelson, leading to a theory that she may have been moved after death. There was no evidence of a sexual assault and no other motive was discovered. Her remains were buried in Caister cemetery. A number of suspects were questioned by police but later released without charge. Several men confessed to Dora Gray's killing but after further investigations all were dismissed as fantasists. Those who still had doubts about Herbert Bennett's conviction believed that a double murderer may be on the loose, though fears that further beach murders would follow proved unfounded.

Was Herbert Bennett wrongly convicted or could poor Dora Gray have fallen victim to a copycat killer? The Bennett case was re-examined in an episode of *Murder, Mystery and My Family* (BBC TV, 2018), which concluded that despite unanswered questions there was insufficient new evidence to declare the original verdict unsafe. The bleak stretch of beach at Great Yarmouth is largely unchanged and still covered with marram grass, though the spot where Mary Bennett was murdered is now beneath part of a roller-coaster ride on a large amusement park.

South Beach, Great Yarmouth, where two murders took place twelve years apart.

THE GORLESTON POLICEMAN MURDER

The murder of PC Charles William Alger sent shockwaves around Norfolk in the first decade of the twentieth century. Born in Bungay, Suffolk, on 2 January 1872, PC Alger was on duty in Gorleston near Great Yarmouth on the afternoon of 18 August 1909, when he was called to a disturbance in St Andrew's Road. Thomas Allen, who was known to the local constabulary as a poacher and petty thief, fired a gun during an argument with his wife. The alarm was raised by a neighbour, Mrs Agnes Cox, and PC Alger was the first police officer on the scene.

When he arrived at the Allens' home, PC Alger was warned by Mrs Allen that her husband was armed and had been drinking. According to eyewitnesses the constable followed his suspect to an allotment at the back of the house, where Allen suddenly produced a sawn-off shotgun and fired it at PC Alger. The officer sustained wounds to his head and face but remained on his feet for several

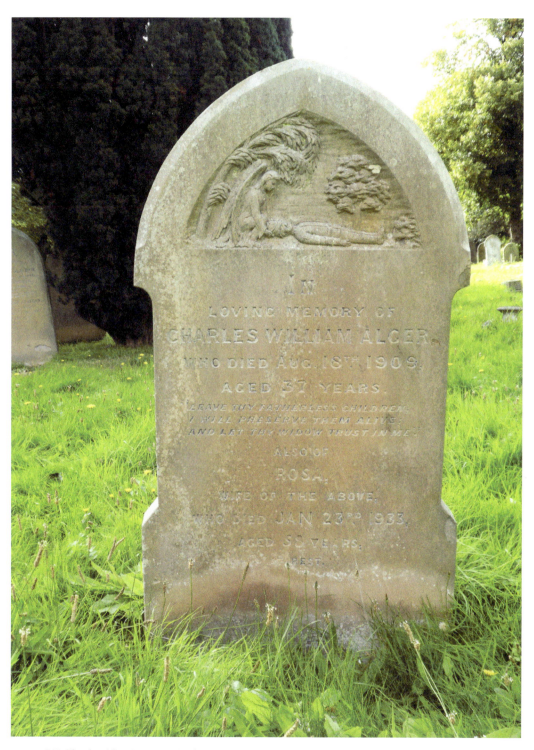

PC Charles Alger's grave, Gorleston cemetery.

seconds before falling to the ground. Allen then went on to threaten neighbours and onlookers and fired the weapon again, narrowly missing one of them. George Warner, who worked as chief gardener at a recreation ground close to the Allens' house, tried to come to the assistance of PC Alger, who was still alive, but Allen returned and fired another shot. The police officer was killed and Warner was injured but survived. After the news reached them, three more officers from Gorleston police station arrived at what was now a murder scene. Inspector Moore bravely tackled and overcame the still-armed Allen and with assistance from PCs Tink and Orford, arrested and charged him with murder.

Thomas Allen was described as being of small stature and looking older than his fifty-six years. At his trial in late October 1909, a jury found him guilty of murder. Following an appeal, the original death sentence was dropped due to concerns about Allen's sanity. Instead he was incarcerated at Broadmoor Criminal Lunatic Asylum, where he died in 1920.

PC Charles Alger, who left a wife, Rosa, and four young children, was buried in Gorleston cemetery. A short service was held at his graveside on 18 August 2009 – exactly a century after he was gunned down – attended by some of his relatives and descendants including three of his great-grandchildren. A wreath was laid on behalf of Norfolk Police.

THE BODYSNATCHERS OF GREAT YARMOUTH

The recently widowed George Beck made a grim discovery in the churchyard of St Nicholas' Church, Great Yarmouth, when visiting the grave of his wife Elizabeth. She passed away on 31 October 1827 and was laid to rest – or so it was hoped – on 4 November. The grave appeared to have been disturbed and Mr Beck's suspicions were confirmed when he and PC Peter Coble dug down to the coffin and found that it was empty. For the rest of November and into December, the police constable kept an eye open for further suspicious activity in the churchyard but without success. His presence may have alerted the bodysnatchers and did not go unnoticed by the general public. It soon became common knowledge that a body had been stolen and relatives of other recently departed folk descended on the churchyard and began checking graves for signs of disturbance. Many coffins were exhumed and at least ten were found to be empty. According to contemporary reports the true figure may have been more than twenty.

The trade of the bodysnatcher, or 'resurrectionist' as he was euphemistically known, was quite a lucrative one at a time when there was a scarcity of fresh bodies for dissection by surgeons. Only the cadavers of executed criminals could legally be used but eminent surgeons often paid bodysnatchers to steal newly buried corpses from their graves. In Great Yarmouth a small gang was employed by the famous Sir Astley Cooper, surgeon to George IV, William IV and Queen Victoria. He made no secret of the fact that he obtained bodies by this nefarious means. Worse still, Cooper was the son of the incumbent vicar at St Nicholas' Church!

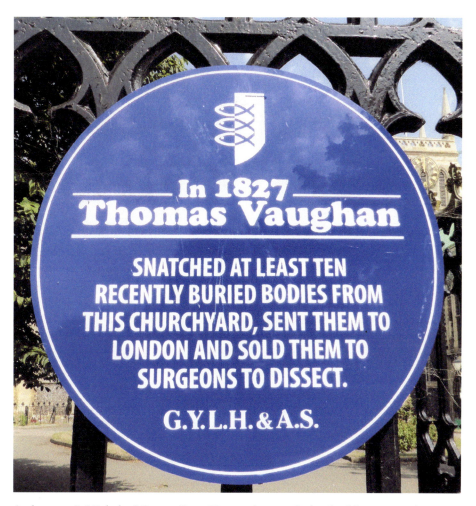

In 1827
Thomas Vaughan
SNATCHED AT LEAST TEN
RECENTLY BURIED BODIES FROM
THIS CHURCHYARD, SENT THEM TO
LONDON AND SOLD THEM TO
SURGEONS TO DISSECT.

G.Y.L.H.&A.S.

A plaque at St Nicholas Minster, Great Yarmouth, records the shocking events of 1827.

The leader of the bodysnatchers was Thomas Vaughan and other gang members included William and Robert Barber and an Irishman named Murphy. Vaughan and Murphy were reportedly paid up to twelve guineas each per body. Vaughan carefully packed them at a rented house in Row 6 – later nicknamed 'Snatchbody Row' – opposite the churchyard before sending them to London. He was eventually arrested and found guilty but received just a six-month prison sentence. Vaughan was later transported to Australia for the crime of stealing clothes from an unfortunate corpse he dug up in Plymouth! The other gang members and their families are said to have benefitted from financial support provided by the London surgeons. Iron railings were later placed around St Nicholas' churchyard to help prevent similar incidents. The events of 1827 are commemorated by a blue plaque unveiled in 2011 at the main entrance to the churchyard.

Other Assorted Tales

THE NORFOLK RISING (KETT'S REBELLION)

This is one of Norfolk's most momentous and bloodiest historical episodes, but it also has all the key ingredients for an entertaining tale. Born in 1492, Robert Kett was a respected farmer and landowner not widely known beyond the small market town of Wymondham (pronounced 'Windham'). The main catalyst for rebellion was the enclosure of areas previously designated as common land. Several landowners, Kett included, erected fences and hedges to prevent ordinary people from grazing their animals there. On Monday 8 July 1549, a group of men started tearing down fences including Kett's. He listened to their grievances, agreed that he was wrong and proceeded to assist them in destroying his own fences. At the age of fifty-seven and a relatively wealthy married man and father, Kett then made the remarkable decision to become leader of the rebels. The very next day he led them on a journey to Norwich after setting off from what quickly became known as 'Kett's Oak' between Wymondham and Hethersett.

The rebels, including Robert Kett's elder brother William, camped on Mousehold Heath overlooking Norwich for almost seven weeks. At its peak the camp may have held over 15,000 people, temporarily outnumbering the population of Norwich itself which housed around 12,000 citizens and was the second largest city in England after London. Visits to Mousehold by the Mayor of Norwich Thomas Codd, the future Archbishop of Canterbury Matthew Parker, and a royal herald all failed to convince them to disperse. After running low on food and other supplies and being refused access to Norwich, the rebels attacked Bishop Bridge on 22 July and made their way to the city centre, where they stole weapons and other military supplies from the historic Guildhall. The mayor and other officials were taken prisoner and held captive on Mousehold Heath.

The use of military force was authorised and a royal army arrived in Norwich on 31 July. More than 300 rebels were killed but the royal army also suffered casualties. Lord Sheffield, its deputy commander, was fatally wounded and died at the Adam and Eve public house, which his ghost is still reputed to haunt. The royal army then retreated and its canons were taken by the rebels. For over three weeks following this victory, Norwich was controlled by Kett's men. A second royal army numbering in the region of 12–14,000 men, including 1,500–2,000 cavalry and mercenaries from as far afield as Italy, Spain and the Netherlands, arrived in Norwich on 24 August. Fierce fighting ensued and over the next

Kett's Oak near Wymondham.

The Adam and Eve public house, Norwich.

A Kett's-eye view of Norwich from the rebels' campsite.

two days several hundred rebels lost their lives. Forty-nine were taken prisoner and hanged at the market cross. The royal army suffered many losses but now held most of Norwich, while Kett's men were still in control of the high ground across the river.

On the evening of 26 August the rebels made the fateful decision to burn down their stronghold and move to lower ground. The final and decisive battle took place the following day at Dussindale, the exact location of which is still disputed. Kett's men, armed with bows and arrows, handguns, a few captured cannons and various agricultural implements, suffered a devastating defeat. Around 3,500 rebels were butchered, many cut down by cavalry as they attempted to escape, while the royal army lost in access of 200 men. Robert Kett escaped on horseback but was captured in a barn in the village of Swannington, north-west of Norwich. Nine of the other leaders of the rebellion were hanged, drawn and quartered on 28 August. Their heads were displayed on spikes along the city walls and around 250 other rebels were hanged outside Magdalen Gates.

After being found guilty of treason the Kett brothers were executed on 7 December 1549, but did not die together. Robert was hanged in chains from the walls of Norwich Castle and his body was finally cut down around three years later. William was hanged from the west tower of Wymondham Abbey. A remarkable reappraisal of Robert Kett's legacy resulted in a commemorative plaque being placed at the main doorway of Norwich Castle in 1949, close to the spot where he was executed. Kett's Oak still exists and the site of the rebel's camp

Norwich Castle, where Robert Kett was executed.

(now called Kett's Heights) is open to the public. It is claimed that Robert Kett's ghost has been seen in the grounds of Norwich Castle and even in the basement of the Castle Mall shopping centre built in the early 1990s.

IMMORTALITY IN WAX

This curiosity was until relatively recently almost unknown outside Norfolk. Today, thanks to the internet, images of the wax effigy of an eighteenth-century country lady named Sarah Hare can be accessed at the click of a computer mouse. The figure is located in the Hare Chapel of Holy Trinity Church, Stow Bardolph, between Downham Market and King's Lynn. It is housed in a wooden cabinet and is sometimes affectionately known locally as the 'Thing in the Cupboard!' Apart from Westminster Abbey, this is the only place in England where a funerary wax effigy can be viewed.

The story goes that Sarah Hare died suddenly after pricking her finger while sewing on a Sunday. On her deathbed she hastily ordered that a wax effigy should be made as a warning to others to avoid this 'sinful' practice. Though this account may be partly true in that she probably died from septicaemia in the manner described, it is known that she organised everything in advance of this unfortunate incident. Sarah Hare passed away in her early fifties in 1744 but left very precise instructions in her will made in August of the previous year. She stipulated that an effigy of her face and upper body should be made in wax and placed behind glass inside a mahogany cabinet. Her highly unusual orders were followed to the letter and the figure wears Miss Hare's own wig and possibly her clothes. Wax moulds were made of her hands but it is unclear whether the face is a death mask. Either way, it is a highly realistic and honest but unflattering likeness. To quote Oliver Cromwell, she is seen 'warts and all'. In her will she stated, 'If I do not execute this in my life I desire it may be done after my Death.' This suggests that the effigy could have been made prior to her demise and that she may even have seen it, though this seems unlikely. Her actual body is assumed to be buried beneath the memorial as her inscription begins, 'Here lyeth the body of Sarah Hare...'

As her decision was obviously premeditated rather than spur of the moment, it appears very unlikely that Sarah Hare meant her effigy to serve as a warning. Her true reasons remain a mystery and it is difficult to guess whether the lady herself would be delighted or horrified that her likeness is still being discussed nearly 300 years later. It is a strange kind of immortality for someone who seems to have

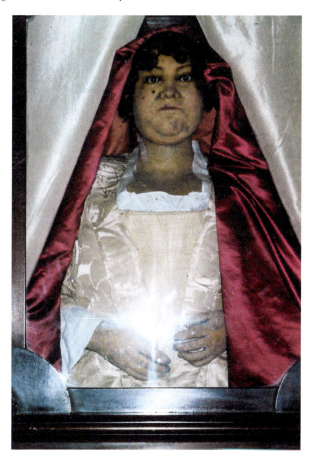

The wax effigy of Sarah Hare, Stow Bardolph Church.

lived a fairly conventional and uneventful life and who would otherwise not now be remembered. Little is known of Sarah Hare's life except that she remained unmarried and was born into a privileged and influential family. For 400 years, members of the Hare clan were lords of the manor and today they rest close to each other in the family chapel. Her father, Sir Thomas Hare and other family members have splendid marble tombs, but it is she who has found a strange kind of posthumous fame.

For the first time since her death, Sarah Hare's effigy temporarily parted company with its cabinet in November 1984. After being painstakingly cleaned and repaired it was returned to its rightful position in 1987. The cabinet is normally kept unlocked during the daytime and visitors can observe the amazingly lifelike image at close quarters.

BRITAIN'S LONGEST STRIKE

The village of Burston near Diss in South Norfolk was the unlikely setting for the longest strike in British history. This was not a walkout by disgruntled employees over pay or working conditions, but a protest by schoolchildren at the dismissal of two of their teachers.

Anne Higdon and her husband Tom were previously at Wood Dalling School near Fakenham from 1902 to 1911, before moving to Burston where Mrs Higdon was appointed headmistress with her husband as her assistant. Having arrived in the village, it was not long before the couple ruffled the feathers of influential locals including the Revd Charles Eland, who in addition to being rector of Burston was also chairman of the school managers. He expected the couple to attend his church services but being chapel-goers they declined. They were sympathetic to the plight of poorly paid farm labourers and Tom Higdon successfully stood for election to the parish council in 1913. Relations between Revd Eland – who was not elected – and the Higdons subsequently deteriorated. Mrs Higdon was reprimanded for lighting the school fire and wrongly accused of beating two girls who later admitted the story was untrue. Despite this, they were both dismissed from their posts on the grounds of alleged discourtesy to the managers.

On 1 April 1914, Anne and Tom Higdon officially left Burston School and were later evicted from the schoolhouse. It was claimed that sixty-six out of seventy-two pupils refused to attend classes and many went on a march around the village waving flags and placards. With the support of their parents, the local children were then taught by the Higdons on the village green before moving into a vacant workshop. After that a temporary building was used before funds were finally raised to build a permanent school. The strike made national and international headlines and the teachers were supported by many trade unions. Burston Strike School was built in 1917 with the aid of contributions and donations from various sources. Violet Potter, who as a thirteen-year-old in 1914 had organised the walkout, declared the Strike School officially open.

Burston Strike School is now a museum.

Britain's longest strike lasted for a quarter of a century but finally ended after Tom Higdon's death aged sixty-nine in August 1939. Anne passed away aged eighty-one in April 1946 and the couple was buried in Burston churchyard, close to their beloved Strike School, which is now a museum. A rally is held there annually on the first Sunday in September. A BBC Television drama titled *The Burston Rebellion* was first broadcast in February 1985.

THE RISE AND FALL OF BISHOP BONNER

Edmund Bonner was rector of East Dereham in Norfolk between 1534 and 1540, before being promoted to Bishop of London. Three connected cottages in Dereham town centre are named after Bishop Bonner and together form the town's Local History Museum. The Roman numerals MDH (1502) are still painted on a gable end, which possibly signifies the year of Bonner's birth.

Known to history as 'Bloody' Bonner due to his ruthless persecution of people alleged to be heretics, he was described as a 'cannibal' by John Foxe in his *Book of Martyrs* (1563). According to Foxe he was responsible for 300 deaths in the space of three years during the reign of Mary Tudor – also given the sobriquet 'Bloody'. Most dissenters were burned at the stake, though some historians believe this figure to be exaggerated and argue that to avoid his own execution

Bishop Bonner's cottages, East Dereham.

Bonner had little choice but to carry out his monarch's orders. When Elizabeth I came to the throne, Bonner was imprisoned and spent almost a decade in jail before his death in September 1569.

THE LONE TOWER THAT OUTLIVED TWO CHURCHES

A mysterious ruined tower stands alone just outside the village of Panxworth, north-east of Norwich. It now serves as a quaint local landmark but over its long and turbulent history has outlived not one but two different churches. Originally part of a large church built in the fourteenth century but later demolished, it then stood alone for 100 years or more before a group of Victorian businessmen financed the construction of a new church attached to it in 1847. Like its predecessor the new building was too large for the local community and after falling into a state of disrepair was eventually pulled down during the 1970s. Since then the tower has stood alone once more and reportedly became a haunt of Satanists in the 1980s. After being damaged by a lightning strike in 2005 it was finally repaired around ten years later. A memorial plaque on the front commemorates ten Panxworth men who were killed during the First World War. Today the site is kept neat and tidy and gravestones in the churchyard are visible once more above the grass.

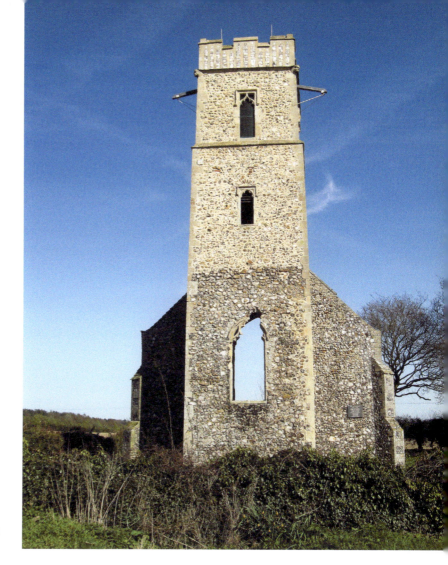

The lonely
ruined tower
of Panxworth
Church.

AND FINALLY...TALES OF GRIM REAPERS!

Visitors to Norwich Cathedral are compelled to consider their own destiny when coming face to face with a grinning skeleton. This is no spectre but a carved stone figure at the tomb of Thomas Gooding, who died after 1625. Mr Gooding was responsible for several Norfolk monuments and requested to be interred vertically inside the cathedral so that on Judgement Day he could spring from his tomb and be the first to arrive in Heaven. His ominous inscription, which includes archaic spelling, reads as follows:

All you that do this place pass bye
Remember death for you must dye
As you are now even so was I
And as I am so shall you be.
Thomas Gooding here do staye
Wayting for God's judgement daye.

For over 350 years, a carved wooden figure of Death stood guard on a corner of a pew in St Andrew's Church, Little Barningham in North Norfolk. The Grim Reaper was draped in a shroud and armed with a scythe. In his other bony hand was an hourglass. An inscription on the pew states that it was built in 1640 by Steven Crosbee 'for couples joynd in wedlock'. It then goes on to warn the living of the temporary nature of mortal existence in a short poem which is almost identical to the inscription on Thomas Gooding's tomb.

Sadly the warning from beyond the grave did not prevent the figure from being removed from its pew around 1995/6. The thief or thieves do not appear to have been apprehended and the Grim Reaper's whereabouts remain a mystery. That is not quite the end of the story as a modern replica was carved and placed on the same corner of the pew that the original once occupied. Though it may lack the gravitas of its predecessor, the reproduction is a fine and worthy successor. When I visited the church in 2002 the new Reaper was still very young but, as the picture shows, looking older than his tender years.

Above left: Thomas Gooding's tomb. (Courtesy of Norwich Cathedral)

Above right: The replica Grim Reaper of Little Barningham Church.

Bibliography

Brooks, Pamela, *Norfolk Ghosts and Legends* (Wellington: Halsgrove, 2008)

Champion, Matthew and Nicholas Sotherton, *Kett's Rebellion 1549* (Reepham: Timescape Publishing, 1999)

Chisnell, David, *Haunted Norwich* (Stroud: The History Press, 2005)

Cooke, W. H., *The Destruction of Eccles Next-The-Sea Norfolk* (unpublished manuscript, *c.* 1914)

Haining, Peter, *The Supernatural Coast* (London: Robert Hale Ltd, 1992)

Howat, Polly, *Tales of Old Norfolk* (Newbury: Countryside Books, 1991)

Jeffery, Peter, *East Anglian Ghosts, Legends and Lore* (Gillingham: The Old Orchard Press, 1988)

Lewis, Charles, *I am myself a Norfolk Man: Nelson, the Norfolk Hero* (Cromer: Poppyland Publishing, 2005)

Mclean, Michael, *Who Was Julian? A Beginner's Guide* (Norwich: Julian Shrine Publications, 1984)

Meeres, Frank, *Paranormal Norfolk* (Stroud: Amberley Publishing plc, 2010)

O'Brien, Rick, *East Anglian Curiosities* (Wimborne: The Dovecote Press Ltd, 1992)

Pestell, R. E., *A Lost Village: Eccles-Juxta-Mare* (Pestell, 1989)

Puttick, Betty, *Norfolk Stories of the Supernatural* (Newbury: Countryside Books, 2000)

Sampson, Charles, *Ghosts of the Broads* (Gorleston: Hamilton Publications Ltd, 2003; originally published by The Yachtsman's Press, 1931)

Storey, Neil R., *Norfolk A Ghosthunter's Guide* (Newbury: Countryside Books, 2007)

Storey, Neil R., *Norfolk Murders* (Stroud: Sutton Publishing Ltd, 2006)

Timpson, John, *Timpson's England* (Norwich: Jarrold Colour Publications, 1987)

Timpson, John, *Timpson's Travels in East Anglia* (London: William Heinemann Ltd, 1990)

Acknowledgements

The author would like to thank the following for their kind assistance:
John and Rosalind Middleton and family; Imogen Smid (www.imogensmid.
com); Philip Thomas, Norwich Cathedral; Joanne Gray, Cambridgeshire County
Council; and Dr Sue Gattuso, Swaffham Heritage.